Remembering

Author writes to honor the memory
of his beloved Mother

REGINALD AUDRICK

Remembering *Catherine*

Author writes to honor the memory of his beloved Mother

Sometimes misunderstood,
but persevered.
Sometimes misunderstood,
but cared.
Sometimes misunderstood,
but loved.
Sometimes misunderstood,
but selfless.

Reginald Audrick

ISBN 978-1-964097-31-2 (softcover)
ISBN 978-1-964097-32-9 (hardcover)
ISBN 978-1-964097-33-6 (ebook)

Library of Congress Control Number : 2022919106

Printed in the United States of America.

To the memory of Ms. Catherine Anderson— devoted
mother and friend of Reginald Audrick, Carolyn Johnson,
and Pamela Acuff.

TABLE *of*
CONTENTS

PREFACE

On June 5, 2017 at the age of 96, my beloved mother was called out of this life to her eternal reward. Like many who experience the pain of losing someone they love, my mind was flooded with thoughts of anguish and thoughts of pleasant memories as I tried to process her death. For days, weeks, even months, thoughts of happiness, grief, and what-ifs filtered in and out of my mind. The woman who had been my mother for sixty-five years, the woman I loved, cared for, and longed to see live until she was a hundred, was no more. She was now a part of my memory bank, stored there and locked away until I take my last breath on this earth. She would also now be a part of conversations with friends, strangers, and family. Her name on my lips would at times cause some misty eyes, and I would have to catch myself in midsentence so that wetness would not become full-blown tears. At other times, when talking to my two sisters, we would reminisce about some of Mama's ways and laugh. Sometimes I would remark to my sisters that something they said, or the way they said it, reminded me of Mama. This would also bring about a laugh and a smile that I could feel over the telephone.

I am not an author by profession. This is my first book about their mother. While I don't remember the exact timing, sometime after burying my mother, I became consumed by thoughts of writing a book about Catherine Anderson, my mom. I wanted to tell her story through my eyes—how I saw and understood her. It would also show how I related to her and her to me. This book represents approximately three years of slow off-and-on writing, along with the editorial process. It is a book that, if God allowed me, I was determined to write and thought it needed to be written. Wow! One might ask, "Needed to be written? Why?" I would respond by saying that in my heart I wanted to honor a woman who, for mos t of her life, suffered through hurt and perhaps just saw herself as an afterthought. Although she is no longer here, I hope people will get to know the Catherine Anderson I knew and will honor her. I want people to know that while she was not perfect, she was a wonderful person who, like many of us, had to deal with scars and disappointments. Hopefully those who read this book will be moved to be a little more introspective. They will consider the wonderful gift they have in their mothers. While many won't go on to write a book about their mother, maybe they can consider other ways to honor her and introduce her to the world.

INTRODUCTION

It is said that daughters are attached to their fathers, and sons are attached to their mothers. Of course, it might as easily be said that fathers have a special attachment to their daughters, and mothers have a special attachment to their sons. Either way, it is assumed throughout human history that there is something unique about the mother-son relationship. No, I do not have any statistics, empirical data, psychological research, or any professional consultants to help prove this point. In my experience, boys have always been fiercely protective of their mothers. Coming up as a young man, it was common for a boy to brag about the prowess of his father but to protect the dignity of his mother. No one crossed the line of offending the most precious female in a young man's life. That person could be a great friend, but she or he had better not say anything degrading about Mama.

I am the product of a single-parent home. My father wasn't in the picture, and I couldn't point to any male who had a continuous positive influence in my life. Many boys who grew up in fatherless homes recall with fondness that coach, scout leader, male teacher, uncle, next-door neighbor, some male who was there to help them through those formative years. There was a Mr. Johnson, a Mr. Kennedy, or an Uncle Henry who served as a father figure. My home life consisted of a mother and two sisters, whom I love dearly and for whom I am eternally grateful. That being said, I can only think of a couple of occasions in which another man affected my life for the better. When I was about ten years old, my uncle Charley took me down to the White House—I was born and grew up in Washington, DC— to see the Christmas tree. It was bitter cold. I can still remember the coat I was wearing and the gloves on my hands. I can still see the reindeer in the cages and the fire bellowing out of a pit, where viewers could stop and enjoy some temporary warmth. I remember my next-door neighbor, Mr. Gordon, from when I was about six or seven years old. For anyone old enough to remember, a TV show titled *Dennis the Menace* aired during the 1960s. Dennis was a lovable young boy whose next-door neighbor was a retired man, Mr. Wilson. Although Dennis didn't mean to, he drove poor old Mr. Wilson crazy. Although I didn't drive Mr. Gordon crazy, I was probably his Dennis the Menace. One day I played hooky from school— yes, even at the tender age of seven or eight—although I am not sure I understood what I was doing. Mr. Gordon saw me, fed me some lunch, took me back to school, and told my mother. Later that evening I was out playing. My sister Carolyn came looking for me, yelling, "Reggie! Reggie! Mama wants you." In those days, discipline meant a good old-fashioned spanking. Yes, my good friend Mr. Gordon had told my mother I played hooky from school. Finally, there was my sixth-grade math teacher. I had a difficult time in school; I was very rebellious. Even in kindergarten, I remember having to go to the principal's office. In fifth grade, school counselors suggested I see a psychiatrist. I recall sitting at the table, trying to manipulate blocks and doing other tests to see what made me tick. The report came back that I was fine upstairs. The guess was that my trouble came from what I mistakenly perceived as female domination. My mother and my sister Carolyn, who is eight years older than me, were always telling me what to do, which was their job, and my younger sister, who was nine years my junior, seemingly always got the benefit of her youth. Boy, I can see the expression on Pam's face when she reads that statement. I needed a male voice. Since I always had female teachers, I constantly rebelled against them. Someone was wise enough to suggest that what I really needed was a male teacher. If my memory serves me correctly, his name was Mr. Roger—with a French pronunciation. I only remember that he was stern and no-nonsense. I remember acting up in class one day, and he took me to task in front of the entire class. I rarely acted out again. As a matter of fact, I consider my time with Mr. Roger as the point at which I noticed I had a certain gift for math.

Without a father or a male figure in the home, my mom was the direct recipient of all my love and attention. I am sure this story can be told by millions of men around the world, yet somehow, I feel mine is unique and needs to be shared. In telling this story, I am trying to help the world know and love a complex woman named Catherine and understand how a man in his sixties still dearly misses this one-hundred-pound, feisty, persistent, driven, and *beloved* woman—yes, my mom—now that she has been deceased for nearly three years.

Chapter 1
AN AWFUL DAY

L ife is a beautiful gift from God, and yet as wonderful a gift as it is, everyone will agree there are good days, bad days and a sprinkle of awful days.. There are days when it is smooth sailing, and then there are days rife with challenges. Bad days are common. Three days out of a seven-day week might be filled with difficulties. Awful days are worse than bad days; however, God, in his love generally only allows us to experience a few awful days in our lifetimes. These are days marked by some overwhelming, horrific event that rocks our world and shakes us to our cores. It's a time of pure hopelessness—a time when everything seems dark. It hits us out of nowhere like a lightning bolt.

I am sure everyone has had at least one or two awful days, if not more. Maybe a call from the doctor containing the *c* word (cancer), a wife or husband wants to end a marriage after twenty- five years, the dreaded call that a close friend or relative has died, or a pink slip that reads "employment terminated." Of course, there are many other earth-shattering events that make a bad day an awful day. Bad days come and go, but an awful day, and its consequences, seem to linger. Its traumatic effects can last for days, months, even years. Fear and doubt consume the individual, leading to questions such as, *how long will the cancer be in my body? When will the disappointment of the divorce leave? How long will it take to heal emotionally from the death of my loved one?* Awful days might be few, but the trauma can last for years.

As a man in his sixties, I can honestly say I have had only a couple of days that qualify as awful. God, in his sovereignty, has spared me from more than that. Please understand I don't know why God has kept me from more of these awful days. It is certainly not because I was deserving or so righteous. If anything, I probably should have had more. On this sunny day in May 2017, I would experience one of those awful days I wish could have somehow been avoided. If only God, in his power and sovereignty, would let me miss this one and maybe give me something else. I wish we got to pick and choose the events that would make up one of those awful days, but we don't. The event I am about to describe came out of nowhere.

My dear mother, Ms. Catherine Anderson, was ninety- sixyears old in 2017, and for about a year or more, she had been the survivor of a fall that resulted in a hip fracture. For a survivor of a recent hip fracture, she was doing well. Still living alone in a three-floor house, she was able to take care of herself. She would get up in the morning and wash up. She couldn't clean herself thoroughly, as her ability to scrub her back or her backside was limited. After the morning wash, she would come downstairs and fix a cup of coffee. Some might be wondering why my mother was still living at home by herself, especially after a hip fracture. All I can say is that she was determined to keep her independence. As long as she was in her right mind, a team of wild horses was not going to pull her from her home. She was a feisty one-hundred- pound strong-willed woman. When her mind was made up, it wasn't changing.

Over the last couple of years, before my mother's passing, I could see her health was declining. I lived with the constant worry that something would happen to her while she was in that house. There were days when I would call to check on her, and the phone would ring more than twice, or she would not answer, and panic would set in. If I called, and she didn't answer, I would be ready to run out the house, jump in the car, and head over to see what was going on.. Then pure relief would set in when I got a call back just before heading out. "Were you trying to call here? I was outside," or, "Were you trying to call here? I was on the phone." Then there were days she didn.t call back and off I went on the twenty minute drive to her house only to find out to my relief that she was okay. Or there would be those times when I would go over to the house for a visit and fear would come out of no where.I was fearing as I went that I would find that something terrible had happened.. When I would knock on the door, and if it took too long to answer, I would in fear use my key to open the door. *What will I find inside?* I wondered. As I was soon to find out the reason my mom hadn't opened the door was that she was in the bathroom or perhaps out back. This played out repeatedly during this stage of her life.

As our mother was now in her golden years, and let's face it, nearing the end of her life, she had lost interest in eating. I would have to always ask her, "Mom, what did you eat for breakfast?" or, "Mom, what did you eat for dinner?" Of course, there were times when I asked her, and she would get irritated and accuse me of acting like a father to her.

The time had come that I had to go over not just for visits and small talk, but I needed to make sure she was eating. I would go over at least once a day and gently let her know I was going to fix a meal. Often this was met with resistance. As previously mentioned, Mom was very independent, even in her nineties. Sometimes she would be in a calm, noncombative mood, and it was easy to fix a meal and have her eat. Other times there was resistance, and this resulted in an argument, or I would have to trick her into eating by promising to eat with her, even if I was not hungry. Many times, I would leave her house with her having only eaten a small portion, and I would wrap up the rest and leave it on the stove. She would promise, "I will eat it later." Although I was disappointed, she did not eat everything, I was satisfied she at least ate something. Part of the problem, I believe, is that I was delusional, unwilling to accept the fact Mom was slowing down, and things were not going to be the same. Meat and potatoes were losing their appeal to her.

It was May 2017. As far I can remember, it was a beautiful day. The sun was shining—no clouds, just a clear beautiful day. It's funny how weather influences a person's mood. When it is beautiful outside, one is ready to conquer the world. "It's going to be a great day!" I am sure I had my day planned. Go over to Mama's house, fix her breakfast, have a cup of coffee, leave and go tend to some errands. It is human nature to plan without assuming anything will happen to alter those plans. We all do it. Unfortunately, there are many days that our plans go awry. Those days when we don't see danger or disappointment lurking. We never take them into account, and as I stated, we are deceived by beautiful weather as if a beautiful spring day was an indication a good and prosperous day awaited us.

On this day, I went over to Mama's. I am not sure if I knocked or used my key, but I entered, and everything seemed normal. Mom seemed well, and we went into the kitchen. She gathered her cup of coffee and sat down at the kitchen table. I had fixed her a light breakfast. I don't remember this as being a day when there was an argument or any resistance to eating. I sat down, and we began to chitchat. Within a few minutes, I noticed her cup of coffee had tumbled over, and without thinking much about it I said, "Oh, Mama, you spilled your coffee." I got a paper towel, turned to wipe up the coffee, and saw my dear precious mother sliding down her chair. The unthinkable was happening. An event was taking place that I thought my independent, strong, tenacious mother would never experience. She was having a massive stroke before my eyes. I actually thought she was having a heart attack. This beautiful day had become one of *those awful* days.

Oh no!! This can't be happening!! Perhaps this is all a dream and I will wake up in a minute. What was happening to my mother is what you hear about with other people. Other people's love ones have strokes and heart attacks in front of them. Other people watch their relatives or friends die in front of them. This can't be happening to me. I am the one normally handing out comments of sympathy because someone else's mother died tragically. But here we are in the spring of 2017 on a beautiful sunlit day and a tragedy is unfolding before me and I can't stop it. Although my mother couldn't talk she seemed to be partially alert which was a tremendous blessing. So here we are,just her and I and the eerie quietness of the inside and outside. There is no time to waste. Immediate action needed to take place. Every second had to be used for the survival of my precious mom.. I do not remember the subsequent order of events. I know I panicked, yet God, in his mercy, allowed me to have enough of my wits about me to try and help my beloved mother. I noticed her stomach swelling. I tried to dislodge whatever was in her throat or just force air up. To be honest, I was just trying anything. Some food did come up, for which I am thankful.

Of course, I called 911 and acted very impatient, thinking all the questions being asked were unnecessary and that if they didn't hurry up, I was going to lose my mother. Later on, I found out that at some point they dispatched the ambulance while they continued to ask questions to better equip the medics to help in the emergency. It is not like they are going to ask twenty questions and then send the ambulance. I also called my beloved wife, who is also a Christian, and in a frantic voice told her what was going on and to pray. I managed to also call my two sisters, Carolyn and Pam. Pam was the youngest. She lives in Missouri, and she loved our mother dearly. She was totally undone, and there was no way for her to be there in the moment. I am sure the wait to hear what had happened and the prognosis was unbearable. My guess is that frustration and a deep sense of hopelessness had filled her mind. While still waiting on the ambulance, I called my other sister, Carolyn, the firstborn, who loved her mother and managed to act a little calmer, which was needed for the situation—somebody had to keep it together. By the way, the medics were there in a very reasonable amount of time, maybe ten to fifteen minutes.

Amazingly, while the ambulance was on its way, my mother seemed to settle down to the point that I was able to settle down. Within about ten to fifteen minutes, there was a knock at the door. I was able to leave mom setting in the chair and answer the door to let in the medics. After a few questions, they checked my mom's vitals and put her in a wheelchair. They took her out to the ambulance, where they further treated her. As they took her out, it never crossed my mind that this would be the last time she saw her house. Mama was not coming back home.

Today we think of two kids as enough and three or four is a large family. In my mother's family seen above there were nine siblings. There are only 8 above. One of the boys is not a family member and the youngest boy had not been born at the time of this picture. Catherine was the third youngest. She is the one with an older sister's arm around her as if there was a special affection for her or the older sister was trying to keep little Catherine in check. My guess is that she was between six and seven. The two parents are also seen. Clara and Andrew Anderson. I never met them. The mother I believe died in her forties.

They say "a dog is man's best friend". While I won't agree with that, I will say that they are special. Even the large dangerous dogs will respond to human love. Apache was very special to my mom. He was smart, protective and gentle. Not to mention that he knew Catherine Anderson was boss. It was a very somber day in our house when Apache had to be put down. He was part of our family and a "friend to my mother".

Chapter 2
MS. CATHERINE ANDERSON'S LIFE

E verybody's life is a story that can be told. There are many twists and turns, ups and downs. There are mysteries to be revealed and some facts to be hidden. Everyone's life has intrigue. There is something the world can learn from our stories. Each of us are made in the image of God, and we are unique to each other. It doesn't matter if a person lived for only a brief moment on this planet or many, many years. There is still a story to be told. Whether the person was rich or poor, Black or white, famous or known only to his or her family, there is a story to be told. Ms. Anderson was no different. She wasn't well known. As a matter fact, she was probably only known to her family and a couple of dozen people outside her immediate family, yet in my eyes her life is a story worth being told. It is not a complete biography but a sprinkle or a dash of what made her life so challenging.

Ms. Anderson's story began on November 21, 1921, in a little town called Jetersville, Virginia. My mother's mother laid on the surgeon's table and was given instructions to *push*. Shortly thereafter, out popped baby Catherine. A pat on the backside and a cry showing that Catherine Anderson was ready to begin her long life's journey, starting in Jetersville. Jetersville is a small town of around eighteen hundred people, located in Amelia County, Virginia. There are only a couple of things I really know about this town: There was one road in, and people had to take the same road out. Anderson was a popular name in the area. Apparently, wild turkeys roamed the woods within yards from the humble beginnings of the Anderson clan. It wouldn't surprise me if my grandfather took out a shot gun and took aim at one of those turkeys for a Sunday or Thanksgiving dinner. My mother didn't live in this small, unassuming town long. She spent only the first four years of her life there. She wasn't there long enough to acquire the famed southern accent. Not there long enough to make any friends. She never talked about anyone from her early life. No funerals to attend of friends she grew up with in Jetersville. Of course, she was not there long enough to be molded by any societal norms or customs. Having been there only four years, she had no fond memories. After she left her place of birth, sometime around 1925, she only got to visit a couple of times during her ninety-six years. As a matter of fact, she only went back when I took her, and those times were at my suggestion. I was more anxious to know about Jetersville than she was, so I took her a couple of times during her senior years. My mother and I differed in that regard. I am a very curious person by nature and have a real interest in the past—namely, things concerning the family. I am a real sentimentalist when it comes to uncovering the past, whether that pertains to others or my own family.

As mentioned above, my mother didn't spend too much time in Jetersville. She told me that she was four years old when her family moved to Washington, DC. That would have been around 1925. It is my guess that my grandfather had made the decision to move his family of nine children and a wife north for a shot at economic survival. Washington, DC, offered as much of a hope as any other metropolitan area north of the Mason-Dixon Line. Trying to feed a large family by working someone else's farm or doing odd jobs was not going to cut it. There was no security and very little income. At least in an area like Washington DC there was the thriving tourist industry, the political scene, and various opportunities for the educated as well as the uneducated. Unfortunately, I know very little about my grandparents. One of the things that is of intrigue to every person is to know their connection to the past. Somehow life seems somewhat incomplete unless we can connect the dots. Unfortunately, I am left to speculate about my grandparents. I have an old black-and-white photograph that is not very good. Apart from that, I am mostly in the dark. I can only assume my grandfather had little to no education and probably worked in some type of agricultural field, like picking cotton. Perhaps he was a little more fortunate and had a skill like carpentry or plumbing. Whatever his employment, it was not sufficient enough to keep him in Jetersville and support his wife and nine children. My grandmother, I assume, was a stay- at-home mom. Considering the times we are talking about—the early 1900s and living in the South—I doubt she had any formal education or employable skills. With nine children to take care of, working outside the home was probably out of the question.

Soon after arriving in Washington, DC, my mom and her family experienced one of those awful days I discussed at the beginning of this book. Her mother died at a very young age— my guess is that she was not more than forty-five years old. I never knew my grandparents, as they had both died before I was born. My mother never talked about any memories she had of her mother. I believe God, in his graciousness, does not allow little children to be overwhelmed by death. I don't think their little minds can understand the gravity of it. It wouldn't surprise me if little Catherine had attended her mother's wake, funeral, and burial, believing her passing was as simple as falling asleep for a season.

My mother considered herself the black sheep of the family. She never used the term *black sheep*, but it is the only phrase I can think of that describes how she saw herself. The black sheep—the one who is different from everyone else, primarily for the wrong reasons. The person who is the black sheep is often considered the bad apple. That person is usually the one who gets into trouble—the one who is disobedient. This person is probably not liked much, if at all. According to my mother, even though she was the third youngest, it was made very clear she was not liked. She shared horrible incidents that occurred in her family, and I wouldn't dare include them in this book. These incidents had embedded themselves in the deep recesses of her soul and would stay there the entirety of her life on earth. I am not a psychiatrist, but it must be nearly impossible to heal scars imprinted on one's soul by others. Be very careful to not criticize anyone who can't "get over it." As I understand it, none of her family members attended her high school graduation. I don't believe she went to her prom. In general, she didn't experience most of the early milestones one looks back on with fond memories. When she was a young girl, she wasn't allowed to be baptized or sing in the church choir, because her family didn't want her to participate. I always knew my mother felt like an outsider. She would often bemoan the fact none of her extended family visited her or called her as she grew older. Now, in all fairness, there was a visit now and then or a phone call from time to time, but they were few and far between. During her eighties and nineties, we would have a birthday party for her, and a few nephews and nieces would come. As a word of inspiration, I want to encourage all nephews, nieces, children, and grandchildren to make time for that elderly aunt, uncle, grandfather, grandmother, or parent. The golden years can be lonely. A phone call, a visit, a lunch, or a dinner can be a tremendous blessing.

I do not know much about my mother's teenage years, except she was pretty, and I assume she had a boyfriend or two. In over sixty years of my life, she never really talked about her life as a teenager. I guess I could say she never talked about it, because nothing memorable happened during those years. It was probably a very difficult existence, based on how she viewed her place in the family. Not only in the family but how she saw herself in general. I do know my mother was very smart and graduated from a very prestigious high school in Washington, DC.

Unfortunately, the next phase of my mother's life did not include college. I have already said this, but I will say it again: Catherine Anderson was very smart. In a different time and under different circumstances, she would probably have gone to college to become a registered nurse or maybe a doctor. Of course, she might have been an engineer or lawyer. From the little I was able to piece together, she wanted to be a nurse but only made it as far as an assistant in a doctor's office. During the seventy years she worked, it was simply a matter of survival. Perhaps thoughts would run through her mind like *Don't let your pride get in the way*, or, *Take whatever is available.* For about fifty years, my mom worked as a housekeeper. That job as a housekeeper showed how deeply Catherine Anderson cared for her children. When a man or woman talks proudly about their responsibility to their family, they might say, "I have a family to feed." Ms. Anderson took a job as a housekeeper, even though she was highly qualified to do other things, because in her heart she could proudly say, "I have a family to feed." I have never and will never belittle that job. If a person can keep a steady job for over fifty years, it indicates he or she is dependable, reliable, and competent. Housekeepers don't make much money, and there are no benefits of which to speak, but all those houses my mom cleaned allowed her to purchase and pay for a house for her kids, send us to nice schools, keep food on the table, and put nice clothes on our back. My mom also had excellent credit. Her generation knew how to stretch a penny.

They were responsible and dependable in paying their bills. I don't know how she accomplished all that she did, but spiritually I can say God was by her side.

Catherine Anderson's adult life was pretty tough. Not only did she have to deal with feelings of loneliness and inadequacy, but she had to raise three children without the physical, emotional, or financial support of their father. Work was often not available, until she finally landed on steady work as a housekeeper. It probably seemed as if the entire world was a dark hole to her. My siblings and I didn't make life any easier, as all of us had issues outside the home that added weight to an already troubled life. Through it all, God, in his infinite grace, gave Catherine Anderson life into her nineties.

Catherine Anderson-probably in her late teens or early twenties. In my eyes she was very pretty, and I am sure she was in the eyes of other young men.

Chapter 3
I DO NOT BELONG

W e live in a beautiful world—a gift from God. When I say we live in a beautiful world, I am speaking in a very generic sense. The world is physically beautiful. God's creative touch is everywhere. Beautiful sunsets, gorgeous sunrises, picturesque mountains, and pristine waters dot our world. Our world is also made beautiful by the many shades of humanity. A wonderful collage of people. Different skin colors and languages all blended together to make a beautiful tapestry. As much as we want to acknowledge the physical and human beauty of our world, we can't be naive and ignore that the beauty is severely diminished by humanity's sinfulness. How much more glamorous would the earth's natural beauty be if humans were better stewards of the planet? How much more breathtaking would the human tapestry be if not for jealousy, hate, bigotry, racism, pride, and so on?

We often think of the breakdown of human relationships— that is, a lack of love—as being between different races or different cultures, but truth be told, the ugliness of human nature can be seen right in the midst of our own families. Some of the most devious and horrific things can and do happen among family members. How many brothers and sisters have made it clear they hate each other? Think about family members who go to their graves having refused to associate with certain members of their family. What about family members who will not attend a family get together if another member of the family whom they don't like will be there. Consider family members who, although late in life, refuse to visit their relatives in a nursing home or who, I am sorry to say, would not darken the hospital door even if that relative was on their deathbed. This horrible attitude dominates them simply because of a misunderstanding or grudge they refuse to let go. I am sure there are people within families who, for no reason at all, just don't like each other. They can't provide a reason why; they just don't. Family members suing each other. Siblings publicly slandering each other. Even crimes as wretched as murder take place among families.

None of this should surprise us. First of all, by nature, humans are sinful. We are selfish. We are bent on evil. Our hearts are callous. We say hateful things, such as, "If you get in my way, I will run you over." Of course, what we see in life now has already been recorded in scripture. Want to see family dysfunction? Please see Cain and Abel, Genesis chapter 4. Read about Jacob and Esau, Genesis chapters 25, 26, 27, and 28. Please see Joseph and his brothers, Genesis chapter 37. This dynamic is also on display in 2 Timothy 3:1–3 (King James Version): "This know also, that in the last days perilous times shall come. For men shall be lovers of their own selves, covetous, boasters, proud, blasphemers, disobedient to parents, unthankful, unholy, without natural affection, trucebreakers, false accusers, incontinent, fierce, despisers of those that are good." Did you notice the "disobedient to parents" in this verse. It is a form of family distain.

In Mathew chapter 10, verse 21 (New Living Translation), we read: "A brother will betray his brother to death, a father will betray his own child, and children will rebel against their parents and cause them to be killed."

Sometimes, inside or outside the family, we are the objects of hate, cruelty, and vindictiveness, and we don't even know why. We scour our minds, searching for a reason. "Did I do something or say something that would bring on the hate?" Sometimes we incur the wrath of someone because they have an unfavorable perception of us, or they don't like the way we look, something that has nothing to do with anything. My mother was like that person who just wondered why she was unliked in her birth family. She once remarked to me that she didn't know anyone who was hated by their entire family. My mother had eight other brothers and sisters. At one point she made a remark to me that gave me the distinct impression she didn't have the certainty she was loved by her mother and father. I am not sure why she carried those feelings up to her dying days. I certainly don't want to deny the reality of what she felt and its cause.

As of this writing, I am in my sixties and for a large part of my life I understood that my mother carried around inside of her this nagging, unyielding thought that she was not liked by her biological family. It was a pervasive thought that seemed to dominate her ninety-six years of life. She just couldn't seem to shake it. The only thing I personally felt I could do was to listen, as there would be times when outside forces and perhaps inner turmoil compressed against this mother of three, compelling her to outwardly lament the fact that her biological family didn't like her. I didn't deny the reality of it. I simply tried to listen with a heart of compassion. I am sure that part of my advice was that she had to move on.

She was convinced she wasn't liked. Indeed, she felt like the loner who just didn't belong. No matter what her children or her friends would say to encourage her, she couldn't shake the feeling of what she perceived as being hated. On many occasions I would remind her that I loved her, Carolyn and Pam loved her, and if nobody loved her, God would always love her. Having said the above, I would never want to say a person's feelings and thoughts are not true or relative. I would not want to say they are the product of an overactive imagination. No one else has a right to deny what another person thinks and feel. We have no right to just set aside the events of a person's life that caused them to feel the way they do. My mother's feelings were very real to her. The events that harmed her were real and not imaginative. While I was not there, I will not sit in judgment as to the authenticity of the events. What a person needs is our understanding, compassion, and some good council. If anything, we need to help a person navigate through situations that might have damaged them. Council them on how to forgive and move forward. Perhaps the best council we can give is to reinforce that while they may be hated or disliked by many people, even those in their own family, at the end of the day the undeniable fact is that the creator of the universe is the one who loves them with an unfailing, unconditional love.

My mother's feelings weren't unsubstantiated. She often spoke of some troublesome childhood incidents. I believe she had a tender heart toward God. She had wanted to join the church choir, but word came home from the siblings that there were too many Andersons in the choir and that Catherine should not be allowed to join, so she was forbidden to join. Next she wanted to be baptized, but again her siblings somehow convinced their parents she wasn't ready. I assume my mother was distraught by this, as she spoke of these incidents until the end of her life. The pastor evidently saw something spiritually at work in my mom, and he baptized her against her parents' wishes. Of course, this might not have been a very wise thing for the pastor to do—that is, go against her parents' desires—but on the other hand, if God had done a work of grace in my mother's heart, then nobody should stop what God may have been prompting. Another incident seemed to come up repeatedly, which in my mind was worse. One of her sisters had prepared some food for a meal. My mom had indicated she would like something to eat. Her sibling responded by saying, "Before I let you have it, I will give it to the dogs."

None of her family attended her high school graduation. No new dress for her high school prom. From what I can tell, there were no happy memories of any celebratory events. I honestly can't recall one moment my mom spoke of with fondness. I can only surmise that Catherine Anderson believed her family in general didn't care for her—the despised one, the black sheep. I can hardly imagine how she must have felt when she went to bed at night, thinking she had no family. What an awful feeling to walk around the house and feel like an outsider.

I wonder if my mother thought the world was her enemy. Now, of course, I don't believe the world was against my mom. At times all of us feel as though everybody is against us. God had brought some wonderful people into her life, but in the grand scheme of things she had very few friends and even fewer romances, all of which went astray, so she never married. She had trouble maintaining friendships, and she often pushed away others with her defense mechanisms. The anger and bitterness she held on to made her life difficult. The Bible tells us there is one friend who sticks closer to us than a brother. I feel confident my mother found that friend in Jesus.

If one can't feed on love from the home, then I am sure they will become jaded and believe no one likes them or, more importantly, loves them. They tend to grow more reclusive and cynical. After all, if not for family, then what's life all about? I need to be clear: I don't know the full story. I can't see into the hearts of my mother's family. I was not a firsthand witness to my mother's childhood trauma. I included this chapter because it is a part of her life as she related it to me; therefore this is a part of her life story. It helps to frame her identity. I love my mom very much, and it became a part of my life's mission to pour love over those wounds.

Chapter 4
JANUARY 1953

I n 1953 Dwight D. Eisenhower was our president, and
Richard M. Nixon was our vice president. The world
population was approximately 4.5 billion people—today it
is about 8 billion. The first successful open-heart surgery was
performed in Philadelphia. Unemployment was about 3 percent.
The cost of a postage stamp was three cents. The New York
Yankees won the World Series. The post–World War II baby
boom was in full effect. On January 31, 1953, I, Reginald Tyrone
Audrick, became a baby boomer. Catherine Anderson was my
beloved mother, and for sixty-five years I would have the love
of this gift from God.

I don't know much about the day or time of my entry into this
world. I don't know about my birth weight. I don't know if my
delivery was smooth or difficult. I don't know if the sun was shining,
or if it was snowing or raining. What I do know is that childbirth is
the first voluntary act of a mother's love. My mother had to lay on
the operating table, and during a short amount of time and with
the possibility of death bring forth a truly miraculous gift of God.
I hadn't given it much thought, but now, as I write this book, I am
thinking that Catherine Anderson gingerly held me for a moment,

perhaps smiled, and then handed me back to the attending nurse. It is possible that during those first few moments after handling me that she began to contemplate the task of providing for me. Generally, this should be a very joyous and carefree time for the mother. Plans would already have been made for the newborn. Clothes had been purchased, the baby's room painted, and a crib and toys all in place. All that is needed is a couple of days of rest and recovery in the hospital and to wait for the father to show up in the family car to carry the little one home. Such was not the case for my mother. What probably consumed her was "How? How am I going to provide for my son?" There would be no father in a car to take her home. There was probably no pre-bought clothes, no new toys or freshly painted room awaiting the grand entry of the new baby. The only thing that awaited Catherine Anderson was an apartrment full of HOW questions.

Today it is common for kids to not have their fathers present at birth. It is not uncommon for kids to grow up without even knowing their fathers. During the 1950s and 1960s, I am pretty sure it would not have been a common occurrence for the father not to be present at the birth of the child and involved in the growing-up years, if for no other reason than there was a societal stigma attached to a deadbeat dad. I have no recollection of my father at any point in my early years, teenage years, or adult years. The only thing I know about my father was what I read on my birth certificate. I knew his first name, middle initial, last name, and occupation (mailman). I have no animosity toward my father. I truly wish we could have established a relationship, even later in life. I even attempted to reach out to him, when I became a married man, but it was to no avail. There is no possibility of that happening now, as he is deceased. The best I can do now is to visit his grave and place some flowers. This is my intention. As of this writing, though, it has not happened.

Please allow me to digress a little here and wax theological.

Life is a precious gift from God, no matter how we got here. There could be no life unless God sanctioned it by putting the spirit inside the body. So, even though I was born outside holy matrimony, God sanctioned my birth while not condoning the act that brought me here. We are known of God, destined by God to be here, and our names are written down in God's book of life. I am also very grateful my mother understood the preciousness of life and didn't seek out some form of illegal abortion. *Roe v. Wade* did not come until the 1970s, which made the horrific act of abortion legal. Over sixty-three million babies have been aborted since *Roe v. Wade* (see www.foxnews.com/politics/abortions- since-roe-v-wade). Who knows what benefit those lives could have been to society. We might never have the cure for cancer or AIDS because it is in the brain of an aborted baby.

I am not 100 percent sure of what was going on in my mother's life at the time of my birth, but I am fairly confident things were not great. She probably had a low-paying job or no job at all. She was single and spurned by another man. With very little help from my father, if any, she was probably very depressed. No matter how terrible the conditions, I am absolutely positive that putting me up for adoption or seeking an illegal abortion was something my mother never considered. Even if Catherine were pregnant in this day and age of freewheeling abortion, and living under the same circumstances that I was born under in 1953, she would never have aborted me or given me up for adoption. So here I sit, some sixty-five years later, writing a book to honor her. There are many reasons to honor a mother. One very huge reason to honor our mothers is that they lovingly allowed us to have life. They chose life over selfishness.

At the time of my birth, I had one sister, Carolyn, who was eight years old. My sister is now seventy-four years old and still has a great deal of memory about my birth and younger days. I would imagine that she would have been excited about the birth of a baby brother, considering she was an only child. As the days went on, and the newness wore off, I became a little bit of a nuisance. My nuisance days probably began as I learned how to walk and began to explore my surroundings. As a little girl, she wanted nothing better than to be able to go outside and play with her friends, but I am very sure she had to keep me under her wing, as my mother was either busy around our apartment, or she was at work.

To this day, Carolyn reminds me of incidents like tying a sheet around myself, getting on top of someone's car, and jumping off while yelling, "Superman!" Or the time she was so annoyed with me that she turned over the baby crib, with me under it, and she sat on it until my mother got home. My sister Carolyn could probably fill an afternoon with stories of her having to watch over an adventurous, mischievous little boy who had no sympathy for his older sister. Carolyn might say, some sixty-five years later, that some of my adventurous ways have not changed. Hopefully I am no longer mischievous.

I am not sure what kind of year 1953 was for me, my mother, or my sister. Mom never talked about it. I had no relationship with my father. I can only surmise that things were a struggle. A single mom with two kids, living in a tiny apartment in a modest neighborhood. I am grateful we stayed together as a family. "Thank you, God, for being gracious to my mother." If my mom were here today, I would thank her for hanging in there. Please don't be mistaken: I have often told her, in print or personally, thank you. For sixty-five years, Catherine Anderson was unconditionally a faithful, sacrificial, and giving mother. I will carry her in my heart to my grave.

The above is a picture of me and my two sisters at a lot younger years. We all owe our mother a debt of gratitude for the effort and sacrifice she made to raise us. As of this writing we are all still living. We are doing reasonably well and stay in contact with each other.

THE EARLY YEARS

W hat would make a man in his sixties want to write a story about his mother? Not just a story about her but have the goal of writing a story that would honor her.

That's a very good question. Growing up, I never experienced special embraces from my mom. I really can't remember any times when she just said, "I love you." I feel as though every time I mention a lack of embraces or not many times hearing " I-love- you", I need to explain to the reader that this lack of emotions was not because my mother didn't care—she cared very much. Perhaps the lack of sentimental hugs or a verbal "I love you" was the residual effect of the harshness she received as a child and as an adult. Her hard and very tiring employment prevented her from attending any sporting event to cheer me on—don't get the wrong idea; I didn't play too many organized sports—and let's be honest, single mothers, due to their very busy lives trying to carve out a life for their children, typically don't have time to attend sporting events. As a kid, we never went on any vacations or special outings—maybe an outing here and there. There was no extra money to get on a train, bus, or plane and go away for a week. I say all this to say that from an outsider looking on he or she might say there is nothing special about my relationship with my mother. Sometimes relationships are mystical. A bond formed apart from anything tangible. Not everyone physically engages a person in a physical manner such as a hug or verbal way such as "I love you", to show their love. Ask a wife or a husband who don't receive those great embraces or soft words of affirmation. My detailing the facts that my mother didn't give those bear hugs or soft words of "I love you" doesn't for one moment make me think she didn't love me. My mother loved me, and I knew it. For sixty-five years I could see her selfless and sacrificial ways to be a blessing to me (and my siblings). Hugs and words are great and should be used but sacrifice and selflessness are better determinants of one's love. My desire to tell the story of my relationship with my mom is the product of my love for her and her love for me. Perhaps this bond developed in the womb and would be there until my mom departed this life to go home to be with her Lord and Savior. This bond endured for sixty-five years and will continue until I leave this earth.

What about the early years that we will call years zero to seven? No, I don't know if I was breastfed or given regular milk. I don't know what kind of baby food I ate; I know nothing about getting my diapers changed. I was never told about my sleeping habits. Did I keep my mother up all night? I can't say for certain. What I do remember is that between the ages of zero and seven we lived in three different locations. The first place we lived was a small one-bedroom apartment on Washington Place in northeast Washington, DC. It was a small two-story building. From what I can remember, the rooms were small. I do remember we had a collie named Lady. I also remember It was here in this apartment on Washington place that I received what might have been my first Christmas present, which I fondly remember to this day. It was an electric train. Boy, that was a very cool toy. There is no telling what that train set would be worth today if I had kept it. My sister was probably in junior high school at that time. As I can surmise, my mother probably had a job, but probably one that did not pay very much.. At that age, I couldn't tell the difference between a good job and a bad job. We had a roof over our heads and food to eat, and we were happy. I do recall that when the ice cream truck came around, and it took a nickel to get some of the good stuff, I didn't have the money. Apparently, my mother didn't have it to give me. Every nickel she had went to take care of her kids. There just wasn't anything left to give. God gave me a sense of contentment because I didn't have a fit. Mom didn't have it, and that was that, although I wished I could be like other kids, handing over my nickel while the ice cream man reached his hand in that cold box and pulled out a Popsicle or Dreamsicle.

I have no doubt my mother wished she had been able to give my sister and I money to buy little treats like other kids, but she couldn't, and she probably felt broken up about it. When that truck pulled up with the bell ringing, Mom looked out the window and saw other kids running up to the truck to buy ice cream. I can imagine her heart sinking as I stood back, only able to look on. After a few years on Washington Place, we found ourselves having to move in with an aunt—my mother's sister—and her son, who lived a couple of blocks away. My guess is that we fell behind on the rent and were told to evacuate the premises. Fortunately, my aunt was available to take us in. Things were tough for our mother. She wanted things to be better, but at this time they just weren't. Please understand that there were not tons of government agencies to get people into a nice apartment or house at a rate commensurate with their income during those times in the late 1950s and early 1960s. So people depended on the kindness of family, friends, and the church. My mother was not a member of a church, and she didn't really have any friends or family to call upon in her desperation. We did have an aunt who lived only a few blocks away. As it worked out, we were able to go and live with her for a short time. I have said earlier that my mom was the black sheep of the family, so I don't know if my aunt welcomed us in with open arms or if it was a matter of pity. I really had never seen this aunt. I don't know if there was open communication between my mom and her. While I don't know, our mother may have approached my aunt about our situation and had to express her desperation.

Moving out of our apartment on Washington Place and into my aunt's home didn't make me sad. I really had no conception of why we moved. All it seemed to me was that we were here one day, in one place, and the next somewhere else. Life continued on. We had food, shelter, and we were happy. There was nothing memorable or extraordinary about our stay with my aunt. As I mentioned above, it may have been the first time I met her, even though we only lived a couple of blocks away. During our stay there, I don't remember eating dinner together or sitting down to watch television together. I have no memories of the place, except for a roof over our heads and food to eat. I am just thankful to God, even as I am writing this book some sixty-five years later, that he made a way.

Our stay at my aunt's place was short perhaps only a few months. My mom was hardworking, not lazy, just sitting around while other people took care of her and her children. Carolyn and I were her kids, and by the grace of God she would take care of us. I said all that to say I am sure her intention was only to stay my aunt's until she could find another place. No plan to coerce my aunt into letting her stay indefinitely. My mom had pride—not in a negative sense—and the last thing she would have wanted was to live off someone else. It wasn't long before she had found us a place to live. It was right in the same neighborhood. The address was 116 Forty-Fourth Street. It was a moderate-looking building in a mixed-income neighborhood made up of middle-class and low-income families. We were definitely on the low-income side.

I have made this point previously, but I was basically a happy kid, despite circumstances beyond anyone's control. Our apartment was my palace. We had no furniture to speak of. For a time, there was only one bed, and I had to sleep at the foot of the bed while my mom and my sister Carolyn slept at the top. Eventually, we were able to get a fold-up cot, which became my bed. We placed it in our empty living room. We did have a kitchen table, but we rarely had days when we would have complete meals on it -in the traditional sense of the word MEAL). This is no slight against my mom. Things were tough. There was no steady work, and when there was a job the wages were meager, barely enough to try to pay the rent and keep some food on the table. Government food helped out: the foot-long box of block cheese, the big can of peanut butter, powdered eggs, and powdered milk. Boy, I hated the powdered eggs, but I lived on slices of cheese and spoonfuls of peanut butter. I learned to be grateful and thankful. As tough as things were Catherine Anderson provided for her family. I don't ever remember going to bed hungry.

It was at this time—around seven years old—that I realized I needed to earn money because my mom couldn't give it to me, and I needed to help out. Yes, I loved playing outside like the other kids, but I also knew I needed to be industrious, and God had given me that type of spirit. I had started to develop Catherine Anderson's trait as a hard worker. There were some early mornings, when school wasn't in, I would rise early, and without my mom knowing it I was out and about, scouring the neighborhood for apple trees, pear trees, peach trees, grape vines, mulberry bushes, or anything that grew fruit. I would fill bags and carry them back to the house, proud as a peacock as I handed them over to our mom. Mother could fry the apples and put milk and sugar with the blueberries. The pears and peaches would just be eaten as they were. By the way, yes, there were fruit trees in DC in those days. It would be difficult to find them today. Too bad kids are missing out on that today and from what I can tell have very little interest in climbing trees.-one of the joys of my childhood.

Another one of my business ventures was collecting soda bottles and redeeming them. Many a time those redeemed soda bottles purchased me candy or doughnuts or ice cream. One moment that still blesses me today was when I woke up early one morning before my mother did. I put on my clothes, got my little wagon, and went out to search the neighborhood for bottles. I wanted to bring home some food to help out. It wasn't long before my little wagon was full of bottles, and off I went to S&R supermarket a few blocks away from where I lived. With those bottles, I didn't buy candy or ice cream, but I was able to buy a variety pack of cereal. For younger readers, a variety pack came in six or eight small boxes of name-brand cereal. The boxes were only big enough for one bowl of cereal, but the wonderful thing is that we got to choose from the different brands. I was so proud. When I got home, I sat the cereal on the table and remember my sister and I getting to actually choose what kind of cereal we wanted for breakfast. I was so proud of being the little man for the moment, providing for the family. It seemed like I always looked for an opportunity to be a blessing to the family. I really believe it was my mom who I wanted to help. Even as a little boy, I just seemed to sense that I needed to help, and I truly didn't mind.

Here I am, all these years, later and there is still clearly one event that sticks out in my mind. We were living on Forty-Fourth Street at the time. I was around seven years old, and my mother was probably in her late thirties. We lived on the third floor. I was usually, like most children my age, outside playing. There would be times that I would be outside playing, and my eyes would turn upward, and I would catch my mother's gaze as she sat in a chair next to the kitchen window. It was something about the stillness, the look of introspection. I often wonder if she was distressed, disappointed with life, or worried about the fate of her family. Often, when things are not going well in our lives, we escape by going somewhere to be alone and to contemplate how we can make things right. I believe my mother was worn out, even as a young woman, and those silent moments at the kitchen window became a place to wonder why things had gone so wrong. Despite these circumstances, she would fight away the negative thoughts and the dark clouds of depression and figure out how to move forward for the betterment of her kids. Isn't that what good mothers do?

Chapter 6
MAMA, I LOVE YOU

M y mother and I did not have a particularly affectionate relationship. On the street, no one would pass us by and think, *Wow, that boy and his mom seem really close.* The only comments we would constantly get, no matter where we were, was that we have a strong physical resemblance to each other. I remember once we were in New York and a perfect stranger said on a whim to my mother, "You can't deny that's your son." On the other hand, people who knew us—neighbors, relatives, friends—knew I cared very much for my mother.

There were no hugs and kisses, no frequent "I love you." There was just an inner desire to see her happy. I loved her dearly and wanted to do anything I could for her. She loved me and my two sisters, but she wasn't the type who expressed it verbally or physically. She would do anything to see me and my siblings have a better life than she did. She would sacrifice her own dreams and desires for the sake of ours. Perhaps all the harsh treatment she received growing up made her resistant to saying or doing certain things such as hugging to demonstrate love. It is interesting that God makes even young children sensitive to the pain others are feeling. Young children can always know when to say something like, "Aren't you feeling well today?" Young children may be oblivious to what is going on around them, but they have a keen awareness for when a person, even a stranger, is having a bad day. Even as a youngster, I was sensitive to Mom's daily struggles.

Those early years were filled with days when Mom was just out of it. Even after things started to get better during the later years, her past still haunted her and tried very hard to bring her down. She either refused to or couldn't let go of her trauma. This is not to criticize her. It is very difficult for any of us to let go of things that have deeply wounded or scarred us. We let them ferment deep inside our souls, and from time to time they raise their ugly heads through fits of anger or rage. Through all this pent-up pain, Mom, by the grace of God, didn't fall victim to alcohol or drugs. I never saw my mother drink, use drugs, or smoke.

Child abuse is another area where built-up hurt expresses itself. How many children have been beaten with no mercy, no concern for injury, because of a parent's uncontrolled rage? How many children have been abused verbally to the point of destruction because of a parent's anger? How many children have been killed because of a parent's violent temper? The parent may have never meant to harm their little ones in this way, but when a person is internally wounded, and that anger comes out, they sometimes lash out at their children. It is as if they are lashing out at the ones who hurt them. The unfortunate thing is that far too many parents who have inner rage don't seek help from friends or professionals. Perhaps pride keeps them from seeking help, or they deceive themselves into thinking they would never hurt their children, or perhaps they have become so hardened they don't recognize the harm they are doing. They don't hear their children's cries or see their sad faces. Prisons are filled with parents who have given into violent fits of rage. Thousands and thousands of kids had to be taken from parents and put under foster care for their own safety. While I will not deny there were flashes of my mother's rage, it never led to any life-shattering scars. Despite her own personal inner turmoil at times and frustrations in general there was never any behavior that would have caused us to be taken from her.

I was sixty-five years old at the time of my mother's death. During those years, I saw times when my beloved mother had come under the sway of rage or anger. What I can also say is that there have been hurtful words said to me, but they were not words that would crush or permanently damage me. I don't remember Catherine Anderson ever saying anything harmful, like, "You will never amount to anything. I wish you weren't my son. I hate you. You are good for nothing." Such harsh words can permanently damage a child. My lovely mom has said things that were tough to hear, but her words never harmed me. Even in a moment of anger or personal dissatisfaction, she didn't use her tongue to injure us. I have felt the blunt end of a belt or switch against my naked backside. None of those beatings landed me in the hospital. They did remind me to never do what I did in the first place to cause the beatings. Today I look back and laugh at those punishments. I think my two sisters would agree that we all saw our mother express rage and anger, but we were never the victims of lasting damage.

Many children grow up to hate their parents. They won't call, visit, send a card, or show any kind of forgiveness. Some children reach midlife, and their parents are close to death, and there has been no contact between them. Their anger controls the situation. They feel what happened to them is unforgiveable. How sad that even as adults their relationships can't be reconciled. I didn't have a walk-in-the-park childhood. I guess I could have found things to be bitter about. But I love my mother. I did when she was alive, and I do now that she is dead. I would like to believe I would run into a burning building to save my mom. I can't swim, but I would like to think I would jump into a lake to save my mother if she were drowning. Any unkind word about Catherine Anderson will immediately anger me. When I left my mother's casket at the cemetery, I only wished she were alive so I could spend more time with her. People have said I was blessed to have had her for so long. I agree, but I wanted her here longer. I don't know how to say it more clearly: I loved her then, I love her now, and I will always love her.

Chapter 7
LEAVING FORTY-
FOURTH STREET

T o be honest, my mother's employment status was very unstable, to no fault of her own. While our financial situation was very insecure, it did not change my mind for one second. My mother was a wonderful mom. I was certain she would take care of us. So, when night came, I knew I would be sleeping under a roof. When dinnertime came, I knew I would be eating something. All the while, though, I am sure she was struggling with concerns about where we would live and what we would eat. There were no food packages left at our door. No friends stopping by to see if we needed help. Only Pam's father appeared a few times and as far as I know none of our fathers offered much if any financial support with the rare exception of Pam's... I seem to remember our mother once saying something along the lines of, "If I have to chase down a man for support, I won't do it." Her thinking might have been that a man is responsible for his children. If he didn't think enough of his children to be concerned about their welfare, then she wasn't going to make him, even if the law would have been on her side.

Before leaving Forty-Fourth Street, our mother had her third child. My new sister's name was Pamela. I assume my mother hid her pregnancy well as I didn't even notice she was pregnant. I just remember my older sister, Carolyn, whom I guess hid the pregnancy from me, receiving a call one day from our mother, indicating she would be home soon, and I was going to have a new baby sister. What a surprise, but a pleasant one, for a little boy. Life is a precious gift from God, even if that life comes into this world outside wedlock. All life is known to God. In some mysterious way, all life is preordained by God. Psalm 139 14–16 (NKJV) reads: "I will praise You, for I am fearfully and wonderfully made; Marvelous are your works, and that my soul knows very well. My frame was not hidden from You, When I was made in secret, and skillfully wrought in the lowest parts of the earth. Your eyes saw my substance, being yet unformed. And in Your book, they all were written. The days fashioned for me. When as yet there were none of them." Think about that. We were inside God's book—or perhaps better understood to mean we were a part of the divine record—before we were born. Ultimately, we were born out of the divine providence of God. Every life is precious.

I am sure that the whispers and gossip was out there, even among the family members. "How could she allow herself to get pregnant again with two kids she can't take care of now? How in the world is she going to feed three mouths? Some people never learn." This is what people do—slander and gossip. The scriptures teach us that real love hides a multitude of faults. No, we don't condone, but we don't spend all day slandering, gossiping, and condemning. We don't run people down. We reach out to help the person who has lost their way. I don't remember seeing any of that. I don't remember seeing any baby presents arriving at our small apartment. No knocks on the door with baby formula or cards and envelopes with cash inside. To be fair, I do have a memory of Pam's father coming over at least once. I still have a little black- and-white photo of him holding Pam on his knees. In general, there was no rush to come to the aid of this woman, who was left with the daunting task of now providing for three young ones.

I need to digress here for a moment. Although my mother had three children out of wedlock, I never saw her carry on in any way unbecoming to a mother trying to teach her children how to live a moral life. There were no men spending the night. No men coming over to the apartment and carrying on. I never knew my mother to have a boyfriend. I never saw her drink or smoke. On the weekends, she was always at home with us. After work she always came straight home. Whatever unbecoming behavior she engaged in was never done in our presence, with the exception of some cursing and angry outbursts, which was probably the result of the pressures and burdens of a single mom bearing the load. of taking care of three children. I am not sure there is anyone who hasn't been pushed to the proverbial limit and let out an angry burst.

Shortly after Pam was born—I would say within a couple of months—there was another event that would in all likelihood push my mom to the limits of her sanity. One very warm day—probably late spring, as I remember—I had come home from school, and all our meager possessions were on the front sidewalk. We had been evicted. Of course, at eight years old, I didn't recognize it that way. I probably just thought we were moving. My poor mom. Every time she got a little settled, bang, something else comes up. I had not yet developed deep feelings of sympathy for my mom. Many years later, when I look back on these events, the sympathy swells up. I thought these were normal events in everyone's life. Fortunately, I don't remember any of my playmates making fun of me or my family, but I am sure the gossip was not lacking. The neighbors probably made hurtful and insensitive comments. Self- righteousness likely abounded.

As I sit here typing, some fifty something years, later it has occurred to me that one of the many wonderful things about my mother is she never created a sense of worry in front of me. Whatever struggles she was having, whether work related or health related, I never knew. I always felt secure in knowing we would have a place to stay and food to eat. So many parents have a way of bringing their children into their problems. The only thing I could know was what I physically saw, and as a little boy I never saw panic. My mother never gathered us around and said, "I don't know what I am going to do." Of course, as I grew older, I had a more realistic understanding of her struggles, and to be honest I became more aware of the frustrations and worries that became a part of Catherine Anderson's daily life. But as a child, I lived in a carefree world.

After we were set out, I found myself across the street at our neighbor's house. This neighbor could be described as a middle-class family. Both parents worked. They had their own house and were raising two little girls around my age—one may have been a little older. They were the picture of stability. My guess is that my mother had to walk across the street and explain the situation and humbly ask if they would take me in for a few days while she tried to sort things out. Who knows, maybe our neighbor, the Bradleys, saw what was happening, and the husband or wife walked across the street and offered to help. However, it happened, I ended up there. I would have a bed to sleep in and food to eat. I am not sure where Carolyn went. My guess is that she went with another neighbor, who was an acquaintance of my mother's. I honestly don't know where my mother and little sister, who was still less than a year old, went. Years later my mother would tell me that she and my baby sister had to stay up all night on a park bench for a day. What a pathetic sight it must have been. A mother with baby in tow and nowhere to go, being resigned to sleeping or trying to sleep on a park bench. What is sickening to me is that my sister's father or Carolyn's or my father were nowhere to be found. We should have never been set out to start with if these so-called men had done what they were supposed to do, which is help to take care of their children. How many people passed her by in the late hours of the evening and didn't stop to help. The park bench that my mother stayed on that night was across the street from the police station. How many policemen saw my mom and the little baby and did nothing to help? It was only the grace of God that preserved my mom during those very trying times.

The next few weeks of our lives would be helter-skelter— staying here for a few days, then moving on to somewhere else for a few days. Mom did everything possible to keep us out of the elements and food in our stomachs. One memorable scene I would like to forget is me, my mom, my baby sister standing in a Greyhound bus station with nowhere to go. Our mother was on the phone, trying desperately to find us a place to stay. I believe that night we ended up staying in a small one-room hotel somewhere in DC. I believe Pam's father paid for our stay. There were no free breakfasts. If we were going to eat, we had to provide for our own food. So, over the next few days, I would take a couple of dollars mom gave me and head down to the corner store and buy a can of potted meat and a can of pork and beans. The beans were eaten cold straight out of the can, and so was the potted meat. This was our dinner. No complaints from me. It was like a steak dinner. There is no doubt in my mind that Catherine Anderson was becoming pretty discouraged. No certainty of where she and her kids would be from day to day, and no money to provide adequate food and shelter. But we didn't go hungry, and we were not out in the elements. My mother was tough, though, and God was a source of quiet assurance for her. How do I know that? How do I know God was a source of quiet assurance? Doesn't everybody say that about their mother? Mom never really talked to me about God in the sense of setting me down for a stretch of time. There were some little sayings about God that she would give me from time to time. As I grew older, I remember every morning seeing my mother in the kitchen with her Bible open and reading. I could've yelled at her, and she would not have lifted her head as she read. Later Mom explained to me that once a man gave her Psalm 91 to read daily, with the assurance that God would take care of her. As I understand it, from the time my mom received that bit of spiritual advice up until shortly before her death, she read that passage. I would like to cite a few verses here. We read in Psalms 91 verses 1–4 (KJV), "He that dwelleth in the secret place of the most High shall abide under the shadow of the Almighty. I will say of the Lord, He is my refuge and my fortress: my God; in Him will I trust. Surely He shall deliver thee from the snare of the fowler, and from the noisome pestilence. He shall cover thee with His feathers, and under his wings shalt thou trust: His truth shall be thy shield and buckler." Let me be clear about several things: I do not believe God is obligated to do anything because we read a scripture over and over. I do not believe we have a right relationship with God because we read a favorite scripture over and over. I simply believe, in this case, that God saw my mom in a humble way reaching out for help, seeking comfort in this beautiful psalm, and in his love and mercy he granted her some encouragement and solace, although she never spoke outwardly of this assurance. In this psalm she found the strength for another day. She gained the push to fight on. Theologians, I believe, speak of this as common grace.

After a few more stops along the way, we made one more - my Aunt Mary's house. Metaphorically, Aunt Mary's was the place where we were able to come out of the rain.

Chapter 8
FINALLY SETTLING IN

I t was the year 1963. For the United States of America, this was a very tragic and somber year. President John Fitzgerald Kennedy was assassinated on November 23, 1963. I was only ten years old at the time, and I couldn't comprehend the enormity of what had happened. To be honest, I am not even sure I knew who President Kennedy was at the time. Access to media was very minimal. It wasn't a given that everyone had a television, so many things could go over a young person's head. I just remember coming home to my Aunt Mary's house one day after school and seeing her crying in front of the television. My Aunt Mary lived in the projects (public housing)—not a lot of money, very little means, but it was obvious she, along with millions of other people, loved President Kennedy. To multitudes of United States citizens, he was the president of the underdog, the forgotten man—the president who offered hope for those who were hopeless.

It was here, at my Aunt Mary's house, where we could finally find a little solace, a little rest for the weary. My aunt was a widow with eight children. I believe six of them were there when we arrived. My mother had seven other brothers and sisters living in the DC area, and we ended up with the one person who really did not have the space or means to take us in. I say all that as a compliment and a statement of gratitude to my beloved aunt. Sometimes the person who has the least to offer gives the most, with an understanding heart and the sacrifice of what little they have. In the bible, there is a historical account of a widow who sacrificially gave what she didn't have. The story was so important that Jesus pointed it out so that some two thousand years later it is right there for us to read. In Mark 12:41–44 (NKJV), we read this: "Now Jesus sat opposite the treasury and saw how the people put money into the treasury. And many who were rich put in much. Then one poor widow came and threw in two mites, which make a quadrans. So, He called His disciples to Himself and said to them, 'Assuredly, I say to you that this poor widow has put in more than all those who have given to the treasury; for they all put in out of their abundance, but she out of her poverty put in all that she had, her whole livelihood.'" I don't believe God is denouncing people who give out of their abundance. I do believe he attaches much value to those who give when they might be in need themselves. All throughout scripture, God encourages us to help those who are in need, even if what we have is minimal. Perhaps we can better view the caring, loving nature of the heart when a person who doesn't have it to give does so anyway because they are concerned. I have no idea how it came to be that we were staying with Aunt Mary. Did my aunt reach out to my mom, or did my mom reach out to my aunt? I don't know, and over all these years it was never discussed. I just know it was good to have a place to come home to and have it feel like I lived there. I was never treated like I didn't belong. Things were also settling for my mom. She found a steady job and a steady income.

I am not sure how long we were with my Aunt Mary. If I had to guess, it was probably a few months. I am sure my mother felt a little awkward being in what appeared to be an already overcrowded house, but when there is a true family atmosphere numbers don't seem to mean much. It almost feels like the more the merrier. One day my mother came home with grand news: we were moving to our own place.

Chapter 9
OUR OWN PLACE

After almost sixty-five years some of my family's past events are no where to be found in my memory bank. . I am very grateful to God for the memory he has given me, but I don't have the recall of a twenty-year-old. To the best of my ability, we had been moving around for about two years, without finding a place to call our own. Living with my Aunt Mary and her six kids was about the closest thing we had to a home once we were evicted from our apartment on Forty-Fourth Street. I know it had to be uncomfortable for my mom while staying at Aunt Mary's. She had to get up very early every morning to make sure she could navigate through a maze of people who had their only early morning agendas; and be on time to catch the bus, and go off to work. While my mother didn't tell me where she worked, and it never occurred to me to ask, I am assuming it was a housekeeping job. I say this because this was her line of work for over fifty years. Assuming it was housekeeping work, my guess is that she had to take those long bus rides to some part of the suburbs of Montgomery County, Maryland, or some ritzy place in DC. My mother was a fighter. She was always willing to take a bus, no matter how far she had to go or how early she had to get up. No matter how unfavorable the circumstances, she would make her way out that door and be on time to her place of employment.

My mother was a very intelligent woman who graduated from a very good high school in DC. As I understood it, the high school she attended was one of the best public high schools in the country. From what I gathered from past conversations, our mom's goal was to be a nurse or work in some other sector of the medical field—I believe she could have been a doctor. Circumstances of the time just did not permit it. None of that mattered now. She had to abandon her previous dreams and ambitions. My mom's attitude was that she had three kids to provide for, and if the only way to do that was to clean other people's houses, so be it. She did not let pride, or a complaining spirit get in the way of her responsibility to take care of her kids. I have no idea where my mother slept at Aunt Mary's. There were my Aunt Mary's kids, my mother and her children (not including Pam) in a public housing unit. To say it was crowded would be an understatement. I slept in the kitchen on a fold-up cot. My mom probably slept on the living-room couch. The point I am making is that she must not have gotten many sound nights of sleep, but early in the morning off to work she went, no matter how cold, hot, or sick she felt.

At some point during the summer, the good news came. By the grace of God, our mother had located a place for us—1302 Saratoga Avenue Northeast, Washington D.C.. I remember seeing the place for the first time. Outside there were pink dogwoods or cherry blossoms growing all over the place. It was a very clean area and mixed—white and Black folks living together. Things were soon to change. Truth be told, things had probably already started to change before we arrived. There were Black and white folks living together, but there was only a small fraction of white people remaining there when we came. My guess is that the area had at one time been predominantly white. We had a two-bedroom basement apartment. I was in the fifth grade, and the good thing was that I was going to have my own bedroom. What a blessing! Our own apartment and my own bedroom. When I came home, I was coming to my own place. I could come in the door, throw down my books, open the refrigerator, grab a snack, and then turn on the television. Or I could just go in my bedroom, close the door, and shut the world out if I wanted. My apartment, my palace!

Mom always taught us to take care of anything or place we had. "A barn could be made to look like a palace" was something she tried to impress upon us. Many a times our mother would be out in the hallway mopping down the stairs that led to our basement apartment. She made sure that both the inside and outside of our apartment was kept clean. This was our home, and she demonstrated as much care for that basement apartment as she did for one of the houses, she cleaned in the suburbs of Montgomery County or the prestigious neighborhoods of Washington, DC.

One of the good things about having our own place was stability. I could attend an elementary school without having to withdraw because we were moving. So, I completed the sixth grade at Noyes Elementary. I also got to make friends, which was very important for a fifth grader. I had a best friend named Orman. I had very good friend who was white, David, and I also had a good friend who was deaf and mute, Eric. I remember those days fondly playing baseball or football after school, or going up to the local market and earning extra money by carrying out groceries for the customers.

One thing almost every little boy love doing is buying his mom something special on Mother's Day, Valentine's Day, Christmas, or her birthday. Of course, what mother doesn't enjoy receiving a gift from her son? Well, I was just like any other boy. It brought me real joy and pleasure to give my special mom a gift on those special occasions. I was able to earn the money to buy the gifts by carrying customer's groceries from the store to their cars or to their homes. There was Buckingham Supermarket. It was one of the real blessings of our move to Saratoga Avenue. It was here that I got my first real taste of making money. Some days during the week, on Saturdays, and on holidays one could find me waiting patiently at the front counter of Buckingham Supermarket to ask customers if they needed help with their groceries. It was a real enterprise for me, as I could make five to ten dollars during the weekdays and ten to twenty dollars on Saturdays—more on holidays like Christmas or Thanksgiving. I was never lazy. If there was an opportunity to make money, I was there. Like many other boys, I also had my paper route. I even loved snow days, as they afforded me the opportunity to knock on doors and seek employment shoveling snow. With money in my pockets and anticipation in my heart after a hard day of carrying groceries, I would scoot over to a drugstore a few doors away and buy that special gift for my special mom. Valentine's Day was pretty easy— just find the biggest heart-shaped box of candy I could afford and have it gifted wrapped. Mother's Day wasn't difficult either. A nice big bottle of perfume or some pretty jewelry. Christmastime was a little more difficult, but it always seemed to come down to some household item—a pretty set of glasses, a lazy Susan, a toaster, or something along those lines. Here I am, in my sixties, and I can honestly say from the time I was able to earn money I don't remember ever missing an opportunity on those special days to buy something for my mom. There may have been times when I only had a card, but it was always a nice card with a special note about what a wonderful mom she was to us. As I got older, into my forties, fifties, and sixties, presents were replaced with going out to dinner or breakfast or having a party for her. Nothing can compare, though, to those nicely wrapped five-dollar gifts.

Chapter 10
A MOTHER'S LOVE

J ust by the nature of her job, a call to motherhood is a call to a very special kind of love. In the Bible, God speaks of three different kinds of love: the Greek word phileo, a kind of love that is associated with friendship; eros love, which is a sexual love; and agape love, which is unconditional love. It is a sacrificial love. It is a love that wants always what's best for the other person, even if it is at the expense of oneself. It is a love that is always giving without expecting back. A love that will die for the other person. When they sing that song "What the World Needs Now Is Love," hopefully they really mean what the world needs is agape love—God's love. I do not know if there is any kind of empirical data to prove it, but I believe God has put that kind of unconditional, sacrificial love in every mother for the good of her children.

Throughout my entire sixty-five years of life, I have known my mother to operate—not perfectly—by agape love, the most special kind of love. A love that is unconditional. A kind of love that can't be squelched. It is the kind of love that would cause a mother to run into a burning building to save her child. It is the kind of love that would make her think her son or daughter is the best child in the world, even if they are in prison for murder. Catherine Anderson believed in me even if others didn't. She thought well of me even if others didn't. She worked tirelessly to provide for me and my two sisters, even at the sacrifice of her own basic needs. I have remarked several times to other people that one of my most precious memories of my mom was a time she refused to buy even a candy bar for herself, as every penny had to go to taking care of her three kids.

There were several incidents that occurred throughout my life that I feel demonstrated my mother's unceasing love for me. I would like to take a little time to share two of them.

When I was about twelve years old, doctors discovered— by coincidence, but really by God's divine providence—I had scoliosis. Scoliosis is curvature of the spine that tends to get progressively worse. I was just a youngster, and I had a mild case, but the doctors warned my mother that unless I did something then to halt it in its tracks I would grow to be permanently hunched over. God had given this young kid a measure of naivety and a noncaring attitude, as I really didn't think much of it and really didn't understand what all the fuss was about. I remember standing in the children's clinic of DC General Hospital with my mom as doctor's discussed with her how they would attempt to fix my spine. The surgery would be experimental. They would stretch my spine until it was straight, or reasonably straight, and attach a titanium rod called a Harrington rod. They would take bone from my hip and graph it around the rod. The surgery would take several hours—maybe it was ten hours or more. What I do remember is hearing the doctors say there was about a 50 percent chance of failure. I could become permanently paralyzed or might even die. Again, I am thankful to God for naivety and an uncaring attitude, as that was some serious talk for my young ears to hear.

Some readers might be asking, "What does love have to do with any of this?" Well, I would say love has a lot to do with it. I am sure Catherine Anderson had to agonize over her decision.

Love asks, "What is best for the other person? If my son doesn't have the surgery, he could become permanently hunched over, always made fun of, never get married, difficulty finding a job." The safest choice was to not have the surgery and hope I never become disabled, but my mother's love was willing to risk the negative because she really wanted me to have a bright future. Of course, if things did not work out, she would have to live with the horrendous thought that she made a terrible decision. Well, as one might have guessed, my mother made the choice for me to have the surgery. The choice was just the start. There would be weeks of making sure I did exercises at home to make my spine loose or pliable. No matter how weary she was she felt the responsibility of making sure I did those exercises every day. Remember: the doctors would have to gingerly pull my spine straight and then apply the Harrington rod. Once the surgery was over, there would be the daily visits to the hospital she would make after working long hard days cleaning out somebody's house. I know of at least one time when she had no money for cab fare and apparently no money for bus fare, and she had to walk from Saratoga Avenue over to DC General Hospital, some five miles or more, and I assume she had to walk back home. Then there would be the around-the-clock care I needed at home in my half body cast. Here I am now, sixty-six years old as I write this book, and never any back pain, with the exception of a few pains due to aging. Other than that, everything is perfect. "Thank you, Mom. Thank you, God."

Another episode in my life that speaks to me about my mother's love was my college education. Every parent wants their child to get a good education, which to most people means going to college. In the Black community, there was probably nothing to make a parent prouder than to know their child was going to college. This would have been especially true as a baby boomer. I am not sure of the statistics and didn't feel it necessary for this book, but it might be that the African American baby boomer was part of the first generation in which it was expected that a child would go to college. We may have been the first generation of African American kids who had a real chance at going to college, and not just African American colleges. We would actually have a choice of where we wanted to go to school. Not only a choice of where we wanted to go but what we wanted to be. That old familiar saying "you can be anything you want to be" was perhaps an unrealistic saying or pipe dream for Black people, but it was starting to become more than a pipe dream for my generation. Being a lawyer, doctor, or engineer was not a full-blown reality, but at least more of us were uttering the words "I want to be a lawyer," "I want to be a doctor," and "I want to be an engineer." Those words had some weight behind them.

The whole idea of college begins with preparation during those formative years. Going to college can be hindered if some proper things don't take place in the home concerning secondary education. My dear mother, although working hard every day cleaning other people's houses and coming home exhausted after catching the bus very early in the morning and having to catch the bus home from work in the evenings, made sure we had a hot meal in the evening, breakfast in the morning, lunch for my younger sister and I, clean clothes for school, and she made sure we were in school every day and on time. This was not to say it was smooth sailing for her going through the educational process. I had both some disciplinary and learning issues early on, but my mom pressed through until I was on the right track. A better statement might be that my mom pressed through until all three of us were on the right track and finished with high school, earning an opportunity to at least consider college, if we wanted. That choice was entirely ours.

To be honest, I do not remember giving college a lot of thought during high school. I probably gave it minimal thought. I really believe I stumbled onto the idea of college. I took the SAT, as probably most of the senior high students did. I scored somewhere in the 900s, which was average. I was a high C or low B student. Somehow, I ended up applying to and getting accepted at Lehigh University, a small private school of about five thousand students, with one of the best engineering programs in the country. When I say I ended up going to Lehigh University, that is not say I don't believe the sovereign God had nothing to do with it. I do believe, in some mysterious way, God is ordering our path to fulfill an ultimate plan for our lives. That probably is too simple of an explanation, but somewhere between my choice and God's sovereignty, I ended up at Lehigh University in Bethlehem, Pennsylvania.

What does going to Lehigh University have to do with my mother's love for me? Good question. To start with, Lehigh was and probably still is a very expensive school to attend. My mother earned probably subminimal wages cleaning houses. I am speaking of minimal wages in the 1960s and 1970s. I am not even sure the federal government had a set minimum wage during that time. I would be surprised if she made more than $1.50 an hour during the 1960s and early 1970s. She certainly couldn't afford to send me there. If my mother could have worked three jobs to send me to college, I believe she would have done so. But Lehigh was a very expensive school, and Mom would probably have had to been a CEO of a top company to have enough income to send me. In all honesty, I firmly believe I went to Lehigh because during the 1970s there was a push to bring more African Americans into these predominantly white schools, even if there were financial stresses. So I ended up getting a couple of small scholarships and a lot of loans. What I learned as an adult was that my dear mom had to put up her house as collateral. Her only prize possession that she worked so hard to purchase with the hope of one day paying off the mortgage and having outright ownership. She thought it was worth investing in me, even though it meant the possibility of losing it by my defaulting on those loans, which were to be my responsibility once I graduated from college. I never knew through my years of college, and even for some time after college, that Catherine Anderson had put her house up for collateral. She never mentioned it once. It did come to a point when she had to tell me because I was very irresponsible about making those loan payments once I graduated, and she was receiving letters and calls reminding her of payments due. To put on the pressure, I am sure she was reminded of the possibility of losing her house. I am very glad for those persistent calls from the school telling me that I must make those payments. Because of my irresponsibility, I might have caused our hardworking mother to lose her house. After all she had gone through in her life and how hard she had to work to keep that house, I don't think I would have been able to live with myself today if I had allowed her to lose it.

Our mother had every reason to wonder if she had made a mistake in putting the house up as collateral. I spent seven years at Lehigh pursuing a degree in civil engineering. The longer timeframe was a combination of academic struggles and getting into some trouble. I never should have taken the path of an engineering degree. I was never criticized by my mother—just letters of encouragement. After finally graduating, I was to partake in a fall graduation ceremony since I didn't fulfill the credit requirement to participate in the spring ceremony. I didn't bother to go and denied Mom the special privilege of seeing her son receive a college diploma. She would have been so proud of me. Once out of college, I got a job with a company called Bechtel as a construction inspector on the Washington Metro Rail System, which was in its infancy stage. That job only lasted about two years, and then I floated from job to job, doing any and everything to keep the bills paid. I am sure Catherine Anderson had many a sleepless night wondering if I ever would be settled and make enough income to insure paying off those school loans. God is merciful. In spite of it all, the day came when the loans were finally paid off, and the paperwork was finally given over that released my mom's house from collateral status. "Thank you, God, for your kindness." Throughout my sixty-five years of life, there were many times when the goodness of God toward me has worked through the hands of Catherine Anderson.

Chapter 11
THE MIRACLE OF
OUR FIRST HOUSE

T he word *miracle* is an interesting word. It is a word normally associated with God, but everyone uses it, both those who believe in God and those who don't. It is normally used to indicate an event that in our estimation, based on natural laws, shouldn't have happened. In my humble opinion, we take way too much liberty in the use of that word. Much like the word *love*, we call way too many things something that it is not. Not to wax theological here, but the Bible helps us to understand what constitutes a real miracle. As I would understand it, a miracle occurs when God sets aside his own laws of nature and creation to bring about an event that would not happen otherwise—God splitting apart the Red Sea so the children of Israel could cross over on dry land, Peter getting out of the boat on the command of Jesus and walking on the water, the resurrection of Jesus from the grave, the raising of Lazarus from the dead, the healing of blind Bartimaeus, and so forth. These all required God setting aside his own laws and bringing about an event that would not otherwise occur. The key here is that God himself is the origin of the miracle.

Okay, so I might be taking some liberties with my use of the word *miracle* when talking about our first house. I realize I may have to really stretch the use of the word, but to a little kid who is now a man in his sixties it seemed like a miracle when I recount how we came into ownership of our house.. During the first ten years of my life, we moved from place to place. For this little boy, joy finally came when we got our own apartment. Please understand that my beloved mother was doing the very best she could. I never thought about or dreamed about living in a house. 1302 Saratoga Avenue was my house, and I was quite content. It really doesn't take much to make a child happy, only some stability.

Somewhere around my twelfth birthday, after having pretty much recovered from my scoliosis surgery, I got a pleasant surprise. We were moving into our very first home, 4207 H Street. For this little boy, there was real joy knowing we would be taking a very big step from apartment to house. We weren't moving in as buyers, but as renters. My uncle Herbert lived at this house as the owner with his wife and children, and for reasons I am not clear about he moved out, and the house became available for rent. I am not really sure why my uncle didn't sell the house, but nonetheless he decided to rent, and my mother's name came up as a possible renter. As I understand it, there was a little skepticism about renting to her. Perhaps there was uncertainty about her being able to afford the rent. I was led to believe my uncle really didn't want to rent to us, but my aunt Ruth talked him into it. I am not saying my uncle was a bad guy, because he wasn't. There is a saying that business is business. If it is true he didn't want to rent to my mother, then it is understandable. Maybe in his thinking he could possibly get a better prospect than my mother, but thank God he gave his sister a chance. I don't think he could have found a better renter than his sister Catherine Anderson—or Sister, as they nicknamed her. She was a hard worker and very fiscally responsible. She would take excellent care of the property. She never put herself before the welfare of her kids, so that rent would be paid on time every month. She wouldn't try to take advantage of the fact that her brother was renting to her and not a stranger. She would keep a roof over our heads no matter what. I am not aware of any one time when my mother missed paying the rent. So thankful that my uncle Herbert gave her a chance. What we all need at times is for someone to just give us that precious *opportunity*.

There is nothing quite like the excitement of moving into a new home. Think about it: three floors to explore! Our small house had only two bedrooms, and one of those would be mine. The other would belong to my mom and my two sisters. As I am typing this, the thought has occurred to me that my mother could have set up a bed in the basement for me or made me sleep on the downstairs couch, but she didn't. Even though herself, Pam, and Carolyn would have to share one room, she wanted the satisfaction of knowing her son would have his own room.

I keep calling this house our own, but it wasn't. It was being rented to us, but to me it was ours. I didn't know nor care we were renting and not owning. As a twelve-year-old, I wasn't really aware of the difference. I had a backyard to go out and play catch with myself and the football. A basement that I would go downstairs and practice my pitching by throwing a tennis ball up against a brick wall. Our house had no fancy furniture. It started off very plain, but I was happy to be there. It would become the Anderson residence for the next fifty years or so. My beloved mom went to work every day, sick or healthy, bad weather or good weather, riding early morning buses to clean houses to make sure we kept our house. She did this until she was about eighty years old.

Perhaps there is one area where our home was not like typical homes. We didn't have many guests, whether friends or family.

Our extended family was somewhat splintered. My mother did not have a very good relationship with her siblings. So, they rarely visited us, and we were rarely invited to visit them. Our mother did not really have any friends—maybe one here or there. On holidays like Christmas or Thanksgiving, we seldom had guests. To be honest, I became conscious of that even at a young age. To me, the holidays were a time when others had loads of family and friends over. There would be laughter and backslapping, reminiscing, poking playful fun at each other, but that was missing from our home. Despite the absence of guests, our mom went all out making sure those two holidays were special. Christmas was the really special one. No fake tree. Rather, we had a genuine evergreen. No table model—a full six-footer. Every year she would pull out the old decorations, buy some additional things, take an hour or so to unwind the lights, and as a family we would decorate that tree. Of course, for our mother, there would be no Christmas in our home without all the goodies. All week long she was a busy baker—chocolate cakes, coconut cakes, sweet-potato pies, apple pies, oatmeal cookies, chocolate-chip cookies, and more, all homemade. Dishes filled with candy and nuts. Then, of course, the outside lights were hung up around the front porch. Mom was busy buying and wrapping Christmas presents throughout the month. All the hard work went toward making sure Christmas at our home was a cherished memory for us kids. For me, every Christmas or Thanksgiving in that house was a beautiful one. Thank you mom.

One Sunday our mother was sitting at home watching television, and a real estate woman knocked on the door and wanted to know why my mother had not been down to the office to apply to buy the house. Without telling my mother, my uncle Herbert was in the process of putting the house up for sale. My mother would have been distraught if we had to move. I do not know why my uncle did not tell her that he was selling to give her an opportunity to buy, but he didn't. Perhaps he just didn't think she would be able to afford the house. I see God's hand in this. While this may not be a miracle in the purest sense of the word, I see it as his loving hand of protection and provision. Though my mother could not purchase the home on her own—housekeepers just didn't make that much—the real estate company advised my mom that she could purchase it if she included my sister Carolyn's salary. So, in a matter of time, my mom, who at times over the years didn't know where she and her kids would lay their heads at night, became a homeowner. What a turn of events!! I don't want to take liberty with the word *miracle*, but I can't help but to think of this turn of events as such. The thought of this real estate woman just up and coming over to our house on a Sunday to inform my mother that the roof over her head was about to be taken away without her knowing it, then encouraging her to pursue the purchase of the house—well, I just see the sovereign hand of God all over it. All glory to God!

Our mother was fearless. She wasn't going to be intimidated by drug dealers or other bad elements that might infiltrate the neighborhood. Anything suspicious like unmoved cars or whispers of drug dealers were going to be reported. Children hanging out in front of her house all hours of the night were going to be reported. You would want my mother as a neighbor if you wanted a neighborhood that could be clean and free of the bad element. In 1979 she was voted in as block organizer. As stated in the certificate above; the mission was REDUCTION OF CRIME.

Owning a house is part of the "American Dream". For a number of years, we moved from place to place. On some occasions we were a step from being homeless, but my mother was strong and determined and wouldn't let that happen. Some fifty years before her passing God made it possible to purchase her own home to which she paid for even though she had very meager earnings. She lived in that house until God called her home.

Chapter 12
MY TEENAGE YEARS

G od did not bless my wife and I with children. I do believe children are a blessing, and the more the greater the blessing. Not having had any children, I can't necessarily speak with authority on raising them. Having said that, it would be my guess that the teenage years are the most difficult years of child-rearing. Teenage years are those great decision-making years—so many things tugging at young people, trying to influence them one way or the other. Those years when they test the deep waters of adulthood. They are not only feeling their wild oats, but they are sowing them, or attempting to sow them. I can imagine that dealing with teenagers is particularly hard when it involves a single parent, especially if there is a teenage male and the single parent happens to be a woman.

My mom was told by a psychiatrist, when I was a little boy, that I had a difficult time submitting to female authority, which was probably the reason I repeated a grade. The psychiatrist was probably right. Having three females in the home and no other male, I was always either being disciplined by a female or accused by one. I am not angry or bitter about that. I love my two sisters and would never have wanted another mother. Whenever I was disciplined by my mother, I probably deserved it 90 percent of the time. When I was being accused by my sisters, I probably deserved it. I was a prankster, a jokester, and a straight-up pain at times.

Mom was a real disciplinarian. Although she was not big in stature, she had a fire in her eyes and strength in her arms for handling objects to wear us out if we got out of hand. She wasn't cruel, but very firm, and she might have crossed the line a couple of times in disciplining us, but again it wasn't violent. Maybe by today's standards it would be over the proverbial boundary line. I wasn't a bad kid, but I certainly remember a few times growing up when I became very aware that Catherine Anderson was not fooling around when I did something that called for real punishment. Of course, being a single mom, she had to put an immediate stop to any bad behavior and nip it in the bud. I can honestly say that in all my sixty-five years there have been only a few times when I yelled at or talked back to my mother, and those times were primarily in my adult years. To use a more informal term, I rarely *sassed* my mother. Talking back to my mother in a way that was argumentative or disrespectful was something I would not have done as a young person, or at the least very rarely. I can say with 100 percent certainty I have never cursed my mother or raised my hand to strike her. Even the thought has never entered my mind. Having said all of the above, I was like many other teenage boys. I did wrong out of my mother's presence and hoped she never found out. If she ever found out, I would simply deny it ever happened. Like most mothers, I am sure Catherine Anderson had an ability to tell when I was lying.

By the grace of God, I reached my teenage years. My mother did what she could as a working single mother, and due to some seeds of discipline planted as a kid and by the grace of God my teenage years were not tumultuous. If my mom were inserting her own comments here, she would say I gave her very little trouble and practically no heartache.

Hoping to not sound self-righteous, uppity, or sticking my chest out, I would classify my teenage years as normal, without much need to be disciplined. I wasn't a partier. I didn't really go to the school dances, but I did go to my high school prom. As I remember, on my prom night, my mom was so proud of me dressed up in my tuxedo. She escorted me out the front door, and I walked down the steps into the car and off to pick up my date. I wasn't tempted to do drugs or drink alcohol. I didn't have many friends. I was pretty much an introvert. I only had a few dates and can't say I really had a girlfriend until maybe tenth or eleventh grade. I was never going to be mistaken for being popular. I wasn't going to walk across the school stage and hear everybody clap. In many ways, my life mirrored my mom's. Although most of what I said above perhaps makes it seem like I had a very dull teenage life, I can say that perhaps not indulging too much into the world has allowed me to see adulthood.

In the previous paragraph, I said I had a normal teenage experience, even though by the standards of the world around me my teenage years might not have been exciting. My mom had raised me not to be lazy about work. I worked very hard. As a matter of fact, I have always found a way to have some kind of job since I was about seven years old. She encouraged me to work by not simply handing money over to me. If I wanted certain clothes or to be able to do certain things that cost money, I was going to have to earn it. So, I have done it all—I hustled for soda bottles, carried groceries to the car for people, shoveled snow, raked leaves, cut grass, worked as a cashier, washed dishes, etc. I would've sold dirt if I thought I could make some money. Robbing someone or holding up a store or cheating someone were never an option.

While my teenage years were far from exciting, they were not abnormal. I was a solid, if not great, student. I wasn't disruptive in class. I worked hard and avoided trouble with the law. Most parents would welcome a child who grew up to be an upright citizen, not a teenage father or felon. As I look back, I am glad I didn't have what the world would call "exciting" teenage years. How many sad stories of derailed lives of those who were told they were "the life of the party" or carried the label as Mr. or Ms. Popular. My teenage years may not have been exciting, but my life has not been derailed. I credit this to God's grace and a tough disciplinarian named Catherine Anderson.

Chapter 13
OFF TO COLLEGE

I n the African American community, parents' desires to see their children attend college were often dreams. Most of our history we were either denied an education or made to feel that at best we could be schoolteachers or low-level government employees. I lived through an era when the opportunities for African American youth to go to college were starting to open up. This was the 1970s. It was not so uncommon for us to go to college, and it became the expectation. It was not only the expectation to go to college but to achieve what was for so long a pipe dream— becoming a lawyer, a doctor, an engineer, or an architect. This was a legitimate expectation. Parents like my mom could really talk about their children going to college. They didn't have to settle for their child working at a grocery store. Even finances were not a stumbling block. College was not just for the rich. Grants, scholarships, school loans, government loans, and work- study programs gave people like me a real shot at going to good colleges and universities. It wasn't a perfect system, but at least I didn't have to say no to college because of money.

In August 1972, at the age of nineteen, it was my time to take part in the dream of many African American kids. I was going off to college to become a civil engineer. My destination would be Lehigh University. To my memory, I was excited about leaving. Going to Bethlehem, Pennsylvania, would be my first time away from home for more than a couple of days. What young person doesn't get excited over the thought of leaving home and being on their own? I don't believe I fully understood that the environment would be quite different from what I was used to. For one, Lehigh itself had under fifty African Americans students out of five thousand, about 1 percent. The high school I came from was the reverse. Maybe ten white students out of five hundred Black students, or about 2 percent. I had never been in an academic setting with more than ten white students. The town of Bethlehem itself was quite a reversal from DC, which was then known as Chocolate City. I am not sure if there were more than one hundred Black people out of maybe a hundred thousand in Bethlehem. Of course, there were probably more than one hundred Black people in Bethlehem; I just didn't see them, because they were spread out or maybe just settled in a few pockets of the city. With all this being said, I was excited about entering this new chapter of my life. I was going to go off to college, become a civil engineer, build bridges, and make Mom proud. My wonderful mother would have been proud of me if I didn't go to college or become a civil engineer. She would be proud as I long as I worked hard and took care of myself and stayed out of trouble. I never had any indication that I needed to do anything other than my best for her to be proud of me. If I ended up being a trash collector, and I was a responsible citizen, she would have been proud of me.

The day finally came. It was August of 1972. The car was loaded with whatever was deemed necessary and probably a few things I did not need. My uncle Herbert was the driver. My mother, two sisters, and I piled into the car, and we started off on the approximately four-hour trek to Bethlehem. There was no big fanfare about me leaving. I don't remember much conversation, if any, about my impending departure. I am not sure there was any special dinner. I know we didn't go out to dinner. My mother had to be very practical about finances. She had very little, so she had no extra resources to spend on special occasions. She always did what was practical. She made sure I had all the things I needed for school and a way to get there. I really don't think I worried myself about anything. I had never given any thought to something going wrong in getting to Lehigh. Catherine Anderson provided that kind of security. All I had to do was get in the car on departure day.

After about four hours of driving, we finally reached the beautiful campus of Lehigh University. My young eyes scanned the campus as we drove up to my dorm. The clock was ticking. It wouldn't be long before I was left alone to figure out my new surroundings. We unloaded the car and hauled my possessions up to the dorm. As I think back on the event, I must have experienced some type of apprehension. I didn't know anybody. No one was running around to greet me and make me feel welcomed. That evening I would eat dinner with people I didn't know. I don't even believe I knew when it would be time to eat or how to get to the dining hall. That night I would fall asleep in a new room with my new roommate- a person I had never met before. Everything was changing so quickly.

Time was passing by, and it became important that my uncle, two sisters, and mother start the journey back. The moment of separation had come. As I said before in this book, my mother was not a hugger or a kisser and neither was I. I don't remember in my nineteen years many hugs and kisses from her to me or me to her. Having said that, I can say Catherine Anderson loved me, and I never doubted that. It was just her makeup that she didn't show a lot of affection. I have no doubt that her lack of receiving affection as she grew up hardened her to showing it. I am confident many emotions swirled about inside her mind. Her little boy had grown up and was leaving home. She was concerned about my welfare. She was going to miss me. As I am writing this, I am thinking maybe Mom did have wet eyes, and there was a hug. All I know is that she loved me. My oldest sister, Carolyn, is not the emotional type either. She is more the level-headed—take everything in stride and don't overreact. Every family needs someone to keep everyone level. Carolyn loves me, and I am sure she was going to miss me, but to my memory there were no tears or hugs. Pam, my younger sister by nine years, was crying. Pam and I, though nine years apart, had our battles—boy, did we have them—so I was surprised by her tears. I can picture her now sitting in the back of the car crying as they began to pull away. That day was about forty-six years ago, and I still remember those tears very clearly. But I can't remember how I felt. Maybe I was fearful. Almost two hundred miles away and all alone. My beloved mother and I were separated. My sisters were gone. No friends as of yet. The next phase of life had begun.

Chapter 14
AWAY FROM HOME

A ny young person who has ever gone away to college knows it is a whole new life. Any parent who has ever sent a child away to college knows this is a whole new chapter in parenting. For the youngster, they are now having to make decisions without the council of the parent. Of course, some decisions are made that the young person already knows what their parents would say, but the student has a new found freedom. He or she might decide to make a choice that is 180 degrees opposite their parent's. They are alone all by themselves. There is no parent to agree or disagree with ; the decision is entirely theirs. There is a lot of freedom in that, but it can also be scary. There are responsibilities that the student has now that he or she may not have had when at home. For example, at college, students are responsible for waking up on time to make it to class. Mom or Dad isn't there to drag them out of bed. Mom or Pop is not there to make sure they get their clothes washed and ironed. It is on the student. Eating properly and getting enough sleep is on the student. Not hanging out with the wrong people or going to the wrong places is on the student. Any decision they make is their own. In the back of their mind, they know what they were taught at home, but the decision is theirs.

Although it isn't always the case, most parents would not want to see what their children do with their newfound freedom. It is like eating hot dogs or scrapple. No one really wants to know the ingredients. Parents probably somehow make themselves believe that all the good upbringing and training would keep their children on the proverbial "straight and narrow." Generally speaking, human beings are not prone to stay on the "straight and narrow," especially when they are young. We want to explore the "wide and open." We want to do our own thing, which while at college was easy to do since there were no parents to answer to. It's easy to succumb to peer pressure. As I said earlier, I led a pretty uneventful teenage life and probably would not have been a candidate for one who would go down the wrong path—my human nature got the best of me also. I was drawn into the same cesspool that everyone else was either already swimming in or would be drawn into. Of course, Mom didn't know. She would have thought better of me. If she did find out, I am sure she would have been both hurt and firm. She would have had a sigh of disappointment and then issued a warning: "You can mess up if you want to, but you are only hurting yourself." Maybe not those exact words, but something similar. She understood very well what came along with not having a college education. She understood that college was an opportunity to escape the kind of economic life she experienced. She wanted a better financial future for me and my two sisters. She had done all she could do. She struggled and sacrificed to get us through very good schools. She presented each of us with an opportunity to have more than she did. Her days were behind her. Her time to achieve economic freedom was over. The best she could do was to continue to work at backbreaking jobs to support us. Apart from working, she could only warn, encourage, and humbly bow to the heavenly Father and ask him to help us.

Now the parent has a different set of issues. The parent had to release the child out into the world and its flawed system. The world into which the child is released can be cold and ruthless. It is a world that pulls and tugs at them, trying to snare them into its web. That parent probably spends many a night wondering how this world is treating their child. No doubt they are anticipating that phone call of something gone wrong. It is human nature. It is how we are. Now as part of parenting there must be a certain amount of trust entered into that wasn't needed in the past. There must be an explicit trust in the child to do the right thing; to make the right decisions; to act in a responsible manner as one who is in that gray area between childhood and adulthood. There must be a certain amount of confidence also. Confidence that for eighteen or nineteen years this child has been trained in such a way that he or she is equipped to be on their own. They are equipped to be in an environment that they had never been in before.

As I said above, I was no different than most kids away from home for the first time. Away from home from the care of my loving mother into an environment that required me to be a grown-up who would for the most part make wise decisions and do what I came there to do: get a college degree. I was to be a grown-up who would one day get a good job, make lots of money, settle down, get married, have kids, buy a house with a white picket fence and a dog, take two weeks off, and use one of those weeks to take the family to the beach. In other words, going to college was to be a smooth sail to fulfilling the American dream. Of course, a big part of that dream was to make Catherine Anderson proud of her son.

My mother was probably no different from any other parent whose child for the first time has left home to be on his or her own some two hundred miles away. She probably for the first few weeks couldn't fall asleep easily. There is a good possibility that she thought about me and worried about me all day. She never came up on the spur of the moment to visit. She didn't own a car, couldn't drive, and had very little money. My mother wasn't an outwardly religious woman. She didn't go to church, and she didn't talk about God on a casual basis, but I truly believe that she prayed for me often. I wouldn't doubt if many a time that instead of sitting, she bent her aching knees and bowed her tired head to a loving God to ask His blessing over me. The letters she wrote often included words of encouragement that God would help me. As my journey through college took about seven years, those prayers were much needed.

Chapter 15
COLLEGE WAS A STRUGGLE

L et me not beat around the bush. From an academic standpoint, college was not easy for me. It was very, very difficult. It took me about seven years—four years full time and three years part time—to get a four-year degree, and to be honest, as I remember, I had to get a little extra push and maybe bending of the rules by a couple of professors to help me. I earned my degree, but it took a little stubbornness on my part. I went to Lehigh University to become a civil engineer. I remember getting around 900 or slightly better on the SAT. Again, to be honest, I really think I got accepted because I was an African American and Lehigh had to show some Black enrollment to continue getting Federal funding. My grades and SAT scores were not high enough to meet the overall standards of the school. Having said that I do think some very highly touted colleges should have built into their programs spots for kids with reasons beyond their control were not better equipped for the academic challenge. Success can't always be measured by standardized tests or grade point averages. I didn't think about the enormous challenge that awaited me as I went after my piece of the American dream.. I didn't give much thought to my preparedness or my ability to get through such a rigorous curriculum. To my knowledge, I never received any council about my career choice or the school I should go to. To this day, I think I made a mistake in choosing civil engineering and going to Lehigh, but I made the choice and was too stubborn to back out when I saw clearly that things were not headed in the right direction.

My class of 1976 had roughly twenty-five African American students. If my memory serves me correctly there were only a couple of the twenty-five who started out in engineering, myself included, who graduated with a degree in that field. I feel fairly certain a great percentage of the white kids went to private high schools, and most of the Black kids went to inner-city high schools. No hard facts about that, just a hunch. I went to Lehigh in the early 1970s. The white kids were beginning to buy those real nice Hewitt Packard calculators and I remember having a hard time shelling out a few dollars for a "slide rule." I had the sense that a large percentage of the kids in my freshman class had taken high school calculus, so college freshman calculus was a refresher for them. I had not laid eyes on a calculus book in high school, also I barely passed college freshman math with a D, if my memory serves me correctly. Many a day I had to hunt around for people in my class or on campus to help me.

Dropping and adding classes went on for seven years, until I finally got the required 125 credits needed to graduate. I finished near the bottom of the class, and we will leave it at that. There was one point when a fellow Black student, a young lady who was a year or two ahead of me, left a letter in my campus box asking me, "What are you trying to prove?" In other words, "Why don't you give up on this Impossible idea of trying to be a civil engineer?" I don't remember how I felt, but that note was certainly not what I needed. I needed someone to take me out to lunch, sit me down, and give me a pep talk. I needed a note saying something along the lines of "I know you are struggling, and I am praying for you." I needed someone to come along and volunteer to help me. Words are very powerful. They can destroy or build up a person. They can be the difference between success and failure. The Bible teaches us this, as does everyday life. The wrong words can start a war. The wrong words can permanently end a marriage. Just a few harsh words can destroy a person's life. The children's saying "sticks and stones may break my bones, but words will never hurt me" may sound good, but that's not true. Sticks and stones may break our bones, and words can definitely *hurt us*. My fellow classmate later either wrote back or told me in person that she apologized. She said she had no business trying to deter me from something I was trying so hard to achieve. She could obviously see the turmoil I was going through, and I am sure she wrote that note out of genuine concern. It was a real struggle for me. I was one of only a couple who stayed in the hunt. I don't make that statement to pat myself on the back, because the wise decision would have been to switch majors. God did not gift me to be a civil engineer.

Seven years in college, nonconsecutive years. Wow! It is hard to believe I dug my heels in that long to pursue a four-year degree. There were semesters when I am sure my grade point average was no better than a one point something. Classes were dropped to be retaken maybe more than once. Most of my major classes were barely passed. For the most part, I gave it my all but just couldn't get past the struggle. I feel pretty certain that conversations were going on behind closed doors about how unlikely it was that I would get a degree in civil engineering, and, yes, I believe those conversations had at least in part to do with me being Black— affirmative action, etc. Perhaps these things were not spoken outwardly, but at least inferred behind closed doors.

Although perhaps some teachers, a fellow student, and perhaps others didn't think I would make it, my mother did. She always sent words of encouragement in her letters, words of affirmation telling me I would make it and that God would help me as I looked to him. I do not ever remember her suggesting I quit, switch majors, drop out, and come home. Never any words of condemnation: "You need to try harder. Stop playing around. Maybe you are not smart enough." My mom was a fighter, a go-getter, one who stood tall against the odds. I feel certain she wanted me to do the same. Seven years? After four years, without saying it, perhaps she was thinking that I should try something else but she wanted me to succeed. She wanted the best for her son. Certainly, after going into the sixth year, she could have been more demanding. "I am not paying another cent for you to stay at that school and fail." The longer I stayed the more money had to be borrowed, and though I am not sure how it works I believe my mom had to continue to cosign those loans to pay for my room and board and to take care of tuition.

The summer of 1979 had arrived. What is so special about the summer of 1979? What is so special about 1979 period? Well, according to the good old internet, Jimmy Carter was our president, the sixty-fifth Rose Bowl was played, we had the Iran hostage going on, and the tragic Three Mile Island nuclear accident. While all those events are noteworthy, for me 1979 was special because after seven years I had finally earned enough credits to get a Bachelor of Science degree in civil engineering. I took my last class in the summer of 1979. It was a surveying course. I had taken the course before but had gotten into trouble on an away surveying camp and failed. That course should have been one I passed the first time. Perhaps there was no one on the planet who believed I could make it, but my beloved mother did. In October 1979, there was to be a graduation ceremony for students who had to take summer courses to earn enough credits to be included the class of '79, which had already held their spring ceremony. I didn't participate in the October graduation. I don't know why. My biggest disappointment for not participating is that I deprived my mother of an opportunity to experience a proud moment: her son receiving his college diploma in an open forum. Even as I write this book, my heart is a little broken that I didn't participate in the graduation, if for no other reason than for Catherine Anderson. I am not even sure I told Mom about the graduation ceremony, and to my knowledge she never brought it up. The last thing I am aware of is that she remembered to acknowledge my accomplishment by ordering me a plaque from the university that stated my achievement. She was proud of me. I still have that plaque some forty years later.

Handwritten Letter of Encouragement
From My Mother (cont. on page 84)

Hi Reggie,

How are things going with you up there. I received your letter & was happy to know that you got a C on your last test. Things are never as bad as they seem, I am sure you are going to come out alright. You ask me to pray for you because you think God will listen to me instead of you because you never go to church or pray. God will listen to any one who come to him & have the faith in him. You must always have faith in God to know that he is able to bring you through all of this. You must always believe in yourself to know that you can make it. So just keep believing and keep trying I am sure you will make it. You are always in my prayers.

I was trying to wait to see if your In come check will come in so I could mail it to you, but so far nothing.

Pam went on a camping

trip Monday for five days, so
I am sure will miss home a lot
to tell when she comes back. I
moved one of your rose bushes
around on the side, it looks nice.
The grass out front looks if it
has never been cut. Well I guess
everything else here is just the
same. So keep you chin up
& ~~get~~ the fourth and I am sure
you will make it.
So take care until we see
you soon,
Love, Mama.

College was very tough for me. It took me four full years and
three years after(part-time). While some three and one-half
hours away from school, there were probably many days of
discouragement and maybe there were times I wanted to give
up. Mama's letters were a source of encouragement. Never
throwing any doubt on me making it even when in her silent
moments she probably wondered. This letter was one example
of her encouragement.

Chapter 16
LET'S GET A JOB, YOUNG MAN

I sn't that the goal? Isn't that the dream? Get a job that pays very well. Every "wet behind the ears" young person goes to college with the idea of getting a degree and hopefully making lots of money. It is part of the American dream. When we were in elementary, middle, and high school, we thought in terms of making enough money with that part-time job to go to the movies, go out on dates, buy the in-style clothing our parents wouldn't buy us, or save for months to buy that broken-down first car. How many young people had paper routes, cut grass, shoveled snow, and delivered pizza, all with the hope of making a few extra dollars. In one way or another, I had every type of job a young kid could get. If there was a way to make a dollar, I found it. I was a worker. A college degree is supposed to create, grand new opportunities. That sacred document says the recipient has arrived. Students are programmed to think that a diploma from a prestigious university guarantees them entrance into the highly sought-after "middle class." In the back of their minds, they have already picked out the house with the white picket fence, the nice new car, brand-new furniture, and stylish suits. On top of that, my family and I will once a year be lying on the beautiful white sands of the Bahamas or in a luxury cruiser drifting along the Mediterranean. Oh, how wonderful to dream! The harsh reality is that the American dream becomes elusive for all too many who come out of college with that degree. For many, the American dream becomes a real nightmare.

I can go back about forty years, to the time I began my post college pursuit of the American dream. I was a senior in college, and it was now time to start interviewing with perspective companies. Every year company recruiters would come to Lehigh. They would review the transcripts and any other documents of graduating seniors. They would set up a date and time for an on-campus interview. Interviewees would put on a nice suit and tie and go to the interview. Somehow, after the interview, the company would do some type of evaluation and decide who would receive a job offer. It doesn't take a rocket scientist to know that the kids with the higher grade point averages had the most companies interested in them, while those like myself, who were at the bottom of the class as far as their GPAs were concerned, did not have as many interviews nor did we get many, if any, job offers. At most, I had two or three interviews with no job offers. I was pretty crestfallen. I had seven years of hard work, headaches, mental breakdown, ridicule, discouragement, mounting debt, and not one job offer. My American dream had started off as an American nightmare.

In May 1979, I loaded up my car and said goodbye to Lehigh University. My academic career was done, and there was no intention of coming back to this school in pursuit of any other degree. The only time I would be coming back would be for sentimental reasons. Over the past forty years, I may have been back a half dozen times. While I left a lot of heartaches, I also left a lot of fond memories. Nonetheless, in May 1979, I was headed for the three-and-a-half-hour drive south to 4207 H Street, Washington, DC. I wasn't expecting any welcoming committees or a party. As a matter of fact, I am not sure anyone knew I was coming on the day I left school. My guess is that I didn't take the time to notify anyone. Of course, my mother was going to be happy to see me ' No, I didn't squeeze or pick her up when I arrived home and set my eyes on her. It just wasn't in our nature to show such outward emotion. We just knew instinctively that we loved and cared about each other. It has been forty years since I left Lehigh University, and my memory may be failing me a touch, but I feel pretty confident my mom prepared a really nice dinner for my first day back, even if she was beat after putting in a long, hard day's work. It was just good to be back to the confines of 4207 H. Street. I was going to have nice homemade meals, a place to sleep, and I would be able to take a good old-fashioned hot bath and not just showers. I didn't have any good job news to tell her. I had no job. I couldn't tell her, "Mom, I got a job offer from US Steel, making twenty thousand dollars per year." I don't remember her questioning me about it or rushing me to get a job. Mom was just proud that I hung in there and got my degree. She could tell people who might ask that her boy graduated from Lehigh University as a civil engineer.

Although I didn't have any job offers at the moment, I didn't feel any pressure from my mother. In my opinion, one of the best traits a good parent can have is an ability to keep the confidence of their child up, not break their spirit. I don't remem ber us having any talks about how to get a job or the need to hit the "streets." There was just a simple quietness that said, "Everything will be all right."

I wasn't just sitting around or running the streets. I was actively looking for a job, and she knew it. I am sure there were many thoughts running through her mind. *Why can't Reggie get a job? When is he going to get that good-paying job?* I am sure she was praying, asking God to help her son gain meaningful employment. Those thoughts would have been born primarily out of her desire for good things to start happening to her son. I am sure she was a little concerned about me paying back those school loans, especially since her house was used as collateral to borrow. The only time our mother mentioned me paying back the loans was when she started getting letters from Lehigh because I was delinquent in making payments. Even then, there were no threats from her, just a reminder that the school could take her house if I didn't make the payments. To be honest, I was not very responsible with those payments and really had a nonchalant attitude. Even with that bad attitude, Mom was gentle and not pushy.

It wasn't long before I got a small return on my college investment. Perhaps it was a couple of months after being home, but I finally received a job offer. Bechtel Engineering offered me a job as a construction inspector on the new Metro Rail system that was being built in the DC metro area. If my memory serves me correctly, I was making a starting salary of between $12,000 and $13,000. Don't laugh. That was a nice starting salary for a college graduate in 1979. That yearly salary seems very low compared to today. Just keep in mind that the cost of living was also a lot lower in 1979. The average income for that year was $16,692. So my salary as a first-year graduate wasn't bad. The average cost of a gallon of gasoline was $0.90. The average cost of an automobile was between $4,000 and $6,000. An average single family new home would have been in the $60000 to $70000 range. All this to say I was riding pretty high, doing all right for a single young man just out of college.

It wasn't long before I got a big fat raise to about $15,000. Then I was really riding high.

It wasn't long after I started working with Bechtel that I purchased a brand-new car, not a used one. I don't remember the make or model, but it was shiny and brand new. I know Mom was proud—the neighbors on the street probably talking and looking.

I was so proud of that car. I would be able to take Catherine Anderson into that new car and take her places she needed a ride to or just out and about for some good old-fashioned relaxation. I remember one place in particular. I took her and my sister up to Sky Land Drive in the beautiful Appalachian Mountains. Mom didn't get to go many places. She mostly stayed home—no trips, summer vacations, or family picnics. She was just never invited or didn't have the means to go. My sister Carolyn always made sure she spent holiday dinners at her house, which was good. She would also get her out on outings with her young daughter, but apart from those times she just didn't get invitations to go anywhere. Of course, Pam was too young to take her places. After becoming a young adult, she and her husband moved to Missouri, where they would raise their kids. I never liked seeing her home by herself, so when opportunities presented themselves, like on pretty summer or spring days or when there were some special events going on, I was glad to plan an outing with her. I remember on many occasions I would call her and ask if she was doing anything, knowing full well she had nothing planned. There were only rare occasions when she turned down my invitation.

Unfortunately, my job at Bechtel didn't last long—about two years.

No job,so no way to fulfill the big part of the American Dream-home ownership. Don't really know why I was let go. I was never given a reason for why I was let go. I didn't make a fuss, so I just assumed they were laying people off, and perhaps it was as simple as "last ones hired, first ones fired." Whatever the reason, I was now without a job and bills to pay. There was the car note, apartment rent, and those school loans. Whatever my mom thought, good or bad, she kept it to herself, and my spirit was intact.

Chapter 17
TIME TO GET MARRIED

A s I mentioned earlier in this book, religion was not something discussed very much, if at all, around my home. My mother, although I believe she had a fundamental belief in God, did not make the discussion of it a major part of raising us. I have no doubt that although Catherine Anderson did not converse with us so much outwardly about God, she consistently raised her heart to God for the needs of her children. Going to church, praying, and reading the Bible were not my personal or family practices. My mother was very private about her relationship with God, although there was one thing she did that I will always remember. She made a daily habit of reading the scriptures. Up early in the morning, before going to work, she would take her seat in that small kitchen on Saratoga Avenue. She would bow her head over the Bible and quietly read God's sacred word. I came upon her one morning as she was reading and decided as a mischievous little boy that I would test her. I wanted to see if I could distract her from reading. Again, it was early in the morning, and she was seated in her kitchen chair, with her head hovering over the scriptures. I intentionally called out in an elevated voice to distract her. Her head did not lift one inch. It was as if I was not there. I believe, though I don't have any proof, this daily reading occurred before then and up until her life ended on this earth. Psalm 91 was her favorite, as far as I knew. That isn't to say she didn't read anything else in the Bible. That particular psalm was given to her during some difficult times in her life and was meant as both a source of encouragement and a reminder of God's favor and protection for those who trust him.

Since I had very little religious education, I didn't know what I believed. Someone could have asked me to name the first book of the Bible, and I probably would not have been able to do it. I wasn't a member of a church and had probably only been to a church service of some kind maybe a dozen times heading into my twenties. I had no religious guidance. I was flying by the seat of my pants. Of course, it is not good to do anything by the seat of our pants. As I mentioned above, I am sure my mother was praying for me, although she never made a big deal about it. I feel confident God heard her cries. I have come to understand that a person might be oblivious to the reality of God. He or she might never pause to wonder if God exists. If they believe in God, they might never acknowledge him when making decisions. Despite all this apathy, God's hand of guidance is still on them. That really speaks to my life. My being at Lehigh was probably his hand of direction on me to fulfill his sovereign purposes for my life. Sometimes we just have to admit, even when we are late in life, his ways are often mysterious. I don't mean this in a condescending way but that sometimes he is working out and orchestrating things that make no sense to us. Oftentimes we really just have to conclude the whole matter by saying, "I don't understand now, and I didn't understand then"'.

In 1972 I entered the academic grounds of Lehigh University. For the next seven years, I would knock my head against the wall over and over again, trying to get that illusive college degree. While I was there I wasn't always studying. I was participating in all the aimless, worthless activities that kids participate in all over the world. At the end of the day, I ended up wondering what this life was all about. At one point or another, everyone grapples with this question.

In the summer of 1979, while I was finishing up my college career, I was coming out of the library from studying for finals. It was the final chapter of this phase of my life. It was a vibrant spring day in May—very bright and beautiful. As I walked down the sidewalk leading into town, where I lived, my path intersected the path of another young man named Marty. Marty was not a Lehigh alumnus. He was up on campus playing basketball and was walking on his way home. God was about to change my life, and Marty was going to be the instrument. As we walked along, he began to talk to me about Jesus Christ and his return to carry his people back to heaven. The point being made to me was that in the grand scheme of things, my own plans lacked eternal value. I don't remember exactly how the conversation went, but I know my ears were open, and God was speaking. Long story short, over the next week or two, I eventually received Jesus Christ as my savior, something each person must do before they die if they want to experience the bliss of eternal life.

It wasn't long after becoming a Christian that I was back home in Washington, DC, and became a member of a small church, Faith Bible Church, located in northeast DC. It was here that I met, fell in love with, and married Frances Taylor. Frances was and still is a wonderful, humble, beautiful Christian woman.

Our relationship was a little unusual, in that she was a widow with a teenage boy, and she was a few years older. None of that mattered. I loved her and wanted to marry her. I believe with all my heart that God had given me a love for Frances. It was his will for us to marry. It wasn't public, but there were at least some suggestions behind closed doors that our marriage was suspect—it wasn't a good idea. To be honest, even my mother wasn't thrilled with our marriage. I say that not to be critical but just as a matter of fact. Every mother probably has a little apprehension about the woman their son is about to marry. But on the other hand, she didn't try to interfere with it. I am convinced and always will be that any disagreement she had about anything in my life was because she wanted the best for me. Nonetheless, we went forward with a very simple marriage, and here we are thirty-seven years later, still married, although there have been struggles. Most of our struggles have not to do with Frances or the slight uniqueness of our marriage, but with me having to grow into a mature husband, allowing God to shape me into the man I should be.

Prior to our marriage, I apparently had made it clear I would be involved in the care of my mother. In other words, I would always be available to help her and do what I could to make her life easier. I don't remember saying that, but Frances to this day will let me know I made that statement or one similar to it. I personally think it is very wise for both parties to have a discussion concerning their future involvement with the care of their parents, especially if their parents are sickly, aging, financially strapped, or single. One of the things among many that I am so grateful for with Frances is that she has always tried to go along with and participate in anything involving me and my mother. Many married women would not want to be married to a man who is committed to the care and well-being of his mother. My mom was very special to me, and I just felt an obligation to do what I could for her at all times, and Frances understood that. Please understand that although I was committed to the welfare of my mother I wasn't going to allow her to have me so cater to her that I would neglect Frances. Frances was my primary responsibility— end of discussion—and I always cared deeply for my mom. A man can do both.

Perhaps I should say here that after thirty-seven years I am trying to be a better husband, trying to not make many of the mistakes I made over the past years. My wife is trying to be a better wife. Some people are further along in the process. I guess I am a slow learner, a little more stubborn. I am glad that God, in his mercy, allows us to improve.

Chapter 18

DETERMINED TO WORK

I was married on August 28, 1982. I had a wife and a thirteen-year-old stepson to provide for. Frances did not work, and it was partly or mostly due to my desire that she stay home and take care of the home. I had become a hard-liner on my understanding that the Bible taught us that married women should not work. Now, after some thirty-seven years of marriage, I have come to believe I was wrong to be so dogmatic about married women not working outside the home. I believe that very careful consideration should be given to the benefits and negatives of the woman working outside of the home. I do firmly believe God has given the man responsibility of providing for his family, and if children are involved that things would be better if the wife made the family her priority. May God give grace for this difficult decision.

I am not a lazy person. Work has always been a part of who I am. From the time I was a little tot, I have sought any opportunity to make money. I have always had a businessman's spirit. I remember as a boy of about seven years old thinking about buying candy and selling it to other kids from a makeshift store, constructed out of boards and cardboard. Collecting soda bottles, carrying out the neighbor's trash; delivering newspapers; shoveling snow and on and on. I was about making a dime anyway I could (legally of course). My mother didn't have extra money to give me, even when we were settled. If I wanted to buy that extra sweet treat, go to the movies, or buy those stylish clothes, I had to earn the money. When things were really bad financially, I remember having to go to nearby construction sites to collect soda bottles and redeem them at the neighborhood store to buy my school lunch for the day. Rest assured, though, our mother always found a way to keep us clothed, food on the table, and a roof over our heads. Once her work became steady, she gave us everything and more. The things provided for us were not on the skimpy side. She wanted her children to have the best, no matter how hard she had to struggle or pinch pennies, but there were those downtimes when she just didn't have any money. Those times probably broke her heart.

Perhaps without realizing it I was a hard worker because my mother worked hard as a single mom, all the way up into her nineties, and I was being molded by her work ethic. Or perhaps it was because my mom couldn't just give me everything I wanted, so I put a demand on myself to work. By the way, no parent should just give their children everything they ask for. What kind of lesson is being taught if our children aren't encouraged to earn money for some of the things they desire? It may take time to earn enough, but it is probably a mistake to quickly jump in and provide for that pair of Nike tennis shoes. Instant gratification should not be a virtue they aspire to. On the other hand, patience is a virtue children should be taught. A parent's soul responsibility should be to provide what the children need. Catherine Anderson did an excellent job as a provider. She, by the grace of God, provided what we needed and on occasion what we wanted but didn't really need. Yes, in my very early years, my mom was unstable in her work. She would have a job one minute, and then maybe something would happen, and she would be out of work the next. I can still see her sitting in a chair at the apartment kitchen window on Forty-Fourth Street, staring out as if she was overwhelmed by the unfortunate circumstances of her life. One of the things that probably saddened her was not being able to keep steady work. I am sure there were circumstances beyond her control. Catherine Anderson was a hard, responsible, disciplined worker. Although the early image I have of my mother's work life was instability, the overall picture I have is of a woman, although very smart and could have held a number of high professional positions, was humbled to do day's work in an effort to take care of her children. She neglected her own wants, and by the grace of God and through self-discipline and frugal spending we made it. Not only did we make it but her three children and a grandchild went on to good secondary schools. Our house was paid off, and I graduated from college. All this to say I had a role model who by example taught me to work hard. There was going to be no lying around and allowing my wife to support us. I had no steady job when I got married. I had a Bachelor of Science degree in civil engineering from Lehigh University, but I had no steady job. I worked for a couple of years with Bechtel as a construction inspector and was laid off. I am not sure why I didn't get another job in civil engineering right away. It may have been that I just couldn't find one, or I was discouraged and didn't try very hard But as I said, I am not lazy. I did odd jobs here and there, and in general I was always doing something to earn a living. I agree that this was no way to enter into a marriage, especially with a woman who already had a child. I had no premarital counseling, but I do believe my pastor was aware I had no stable income. He was not really all in for the marriage. Nonetheless, we went ahead with the marriage, and now I had the responsibility of earning enough money to take care of the household.

Above I mentioned the elusive American dream: go to college, graduate, and come out making lots of money. Well, it didn't work that way for me. Although I had a degree in civil engineering from a prestigious college, I had no prestigious job. I am almost ashamed to say that for a great portion of my married life I had to piece together jobs. I needed to earn a living, and I wasn't going to wait around to get that money as a civil engineer. Pride wasn't going to get in the way. I was willing to take a job doing anything legal and honorable that would earn me enough money at the end of the day—yard work, painting, laying cable, and anything else that had dollar signs attached to it. I remember catching the bus with my hedge trimmers to go somewhere out in the suburbs to do yard work.

I know my mother was disappointed. Perhaps I shouldn't say that. I should say I assume she was disappointed—disappointed that I didn't secure one of those well-paying engineering jobs. Disappointed that her college-educated son was making a living by cutting people's grass, raking their leaves, and painting their houses. No matter how disappointed she may have been, she never let me know. She was just glad I was working and not out robbing banks. She was proud of her son, the college graduate.

Chapter 19
WHY NOT START
A BUSINESS?

C utting grass, raking leaves, painting houses, anything to make money in an effort to keep food on the table and pay the rent, along with other bills. Of course, this wasn't going to do in the long run, and it was too iffy. I had an entrepreneurial spirit, and I was and still am a dreamer. I don't remember how it all happened, but the idea came to me to start a tutorial service. I was out of sustainable work, and I needed to put any God-given gift to work to support my family. The truth is that whatever I was doing I had in the back of my mind that it was going to someday net lots of profit. The other truth is that what I was doing was not going to get me there. I had some fairly good academic skills, especially for math. There was a need for my service. I crunched the numbers and thought I could make a good living, so it was off to the races. I got some flash cards, slips of paper, made a low cost, handwritten advertisement and started sliding them under doors. Before I knew it, I was gaining customers, and I was seeing the potential. I applied for a business license, and RA Educational Services was born. Even though I didn't have a business plan, nor consulted with anyone, I just knew it would be a matter of time before my in-home tutorial service had centers all over the DC metro area and in other states. Yes, I was going to be a millionaire. One thing I have never lacked was optimism and the ability to dream. I really thought it was just a matter of distributing enough business cards and flyers. At one point I had it down to a science—every thousand fliers distributed would generate eight new clients. That was the goal.

At the time of the start of my tutorial service, my wife and I were living in a rented apartment. As a Christian, it wasn't difficult for me to sense I was doing something wrong, and my conscience would start to bother me. It was not right for me to operate a licensed business from my rented apartment, at least the way I understood it. Maybe there was some technicality that would allow me to do it, but it just didn't appear right. I needed a business phone and a business address, yet it was not part of my rental agreement that I could do this. No business could be legitimate without an address and a phone number, yet I did not want to violate my conscience and do what I believed to be wrong by operating a business out of my apartment. The solution laid with the person who birthed me into this world, the person who did not mock my dreams or cast me down for my failures: my mother, Ms. Catherine Anderson. She owned a home. I could set up the business phone on a separate line from her house and also use her house number as the business address. Problem solved.

When I asked her to let me put in a separate line for the business and use her address as the business address, there were no lectures, no questions about the possibility of failure, and no negotiations about money. Whatever doubts she may have had, she kept to herself. From the bottom of my heart, I believe that as a parent the most important thing our mother wanted was for us to succeed. She believed in us and would do anything to bring our success to fruition. In the back of her mind, or deep inside her heart, she probably really wanted me to be an engineer, but she didn't let on. At the end of the day, she just wanted more for us than what she had gotten out of life. Isn't that what any good parent would want for their children? My business was my dream, and she was probably convinced I would become successful in this venture. There were many, many tutorial services out there, but her son would still make it. For about thirty years, more or less, 4207 H Street was the address of RA Educational Services, and 202-610-1460 was the phone number. Thank you, Mom.

Chapter 20
MY MOTHER,
MY SECRETARY

Hiring a secretary is a major step for any new business. Many businesses that hire their first secretary or office manager are really going to be out of business in a year or two; however, if a business is going to have an opportunity to grow, they at least need a competent secretary. Well, for me to start out, my phone voice mail was my secretary. People would call and leave a message, and I would retrieve that message later on and call them back. Of course, the problem with that was that if someone called looking for a service there is at least a good possibility they want to close the deal right then and there. If no one is there to close the deal, then they might leave a message but would maybe go on to try some other company. My business started during the mid-1990s, and emails, text messages, and cell phones were not the norm. Good old landline phones, snail mail, faxes, and pagers were the general forms of communication.

At the time when all this was taking place, my mom was in her early to mid-sixties. She was still getting up early in the morning to catch a bus to her employer's house as a housekeeper. Sixty something isn't ancient, but when someone is getting up early, walking to the bus stop about five blocks away, and then having to transfer to other buses to go out to a Maryland suburb some ten miles away, clean somebody's house, and then make the long trek back home, they are exhausted. Not to mention that my mom had to take care of a dog, raise a grandchild, clean her own house, and do other things that required her attention. Our poor mother. Here she is, in her sixties and approaching the grand old number seventy. At her age, she should have been able to retire and enjoy the fruits of her labor, just like many people aspire to do. It would have been nice after approximately fifty years of toil if she could have come home and done some of the things she wanted to do. Perhaps she could have just laid in bed until she was ready to get up. Maybe she would have enjoyed puttering around the yard, as she loved her flowers. Maybe she would have been able to go on a cruise. None of these things were happened. There was no retirement pay, no annuities, and no 401(k). There was only a few hundred dollars a month from social security. It isn't easy to live on several hundred dollars a month, even if the house is paid for. It is nearly impossible. So, our precious mom had to work into her eighties—and into her nineties, helping me with RA Educational Services.

In spite of the hectic and very tiresome schedule my mother carried, I did what could be considered somewhat selfish. I asked her if she would check the phone to see if any calls came in, write them down, and call the people back. I also asked her if she would answer the phone when she was available.

I can still hear her voice today. "RA, how may I help you?" For some reason, she wouldn't say the complete name of the company, RA Educational Services. She had a very calming and pleasant voice and oftentimes would enter into belly laughs as parents told stories of how frustrated they were with trying to get good grades from their children. There were also those times when she would give sage advice. My mother would get home around three or four o'clock, as I recall, and so there was still a couple of hours until six. She could have said, "Reggie, I am too tired when I come home." She could have said, "You are asking too much of me." No, she didn't say any of that. She just agreed to do it.

What started out just answering the phone led to more and more responsibilities, until I didn't have a secretary. I had an office manager. When the business first started, I was doing all the tutoring, but as more and more people started to call and desire a tutor, I couldn't do it all myself, and there were some subjects I just didn't know. Sorry, but I didn't know French, and I wasn't good at classical literature, and even some math was a little beyond my boundary. I needed help! So, my mother's function now involved receiving résumés and calling potential tutors. Once new tutors were hired, my mother not only returned calls to new clients but paired a tutor with the client.

The tasks continued to grow for my mother. She returned calls, took new calls, was instrumental in hiring new tutors, assigned tutors to clients, and now she had to become an accountant. That's right—she kept the books. She had to record money coming in and money going out, as far as tutor's salaries, and at the end of the year give me a total made and a total spent, as far as salaries. Don't be fooled. As I have said several times already, Catherine Anderson cleaned houses for a living out of necessity, but she was very bright. Under different circumstances she could have been a registered nurse, a doctor, a lawyer, or any number of other highly skilled professions. Sometimes I wonder if God didn't allow Ms. Anderson to use her God-given skills until a later stage of life as a reminder she was gifted. He was giving her a temporal reward toward the later stage of life. Actually, I feel the same way about my life. I went to school to be a civil engineer but was unsuccessful. I had to make a living raking leaves, painting houses, and cutting grass. Yet God, in his kindness and mercy, has allowed me to find a way that I could use my God-given skill of working with math to secure a proper living for my family.

There was no way I could afford a secretary or office manager. I needed one or the other or maybe both, but I could not afford it. My mom has been a mainstay in my life, always willing to help without asking for anything in return. I wasn't going to take advantage of her willingness to help without paying her something. I know she was struggling to make ends meet. I needed to do what was right. I wanted to pay my mother $300 to $500 a week, but it just didn't happen. I was barely making enough to live on and pay the tutors. Unfortunately, I was doing well enough to pay her maybe $400 to $500 per month. Was she worth more? Absolutely! I was hoping the day was going to come when I could pay her a real yearly salary—maybe $30,000 to $40,000. It never happened, but that extra few thousand dollars came in handy, especially in her elderly years. Sadly, as the years went on and RA Educational Services began to flounder, I was barely able to pay her anything. It got to the point where the business was only a business on paper. This coincided with the demise of Ms. Anderson's health. Her bills were still there, and she needed the money. There were times when I really didn't have anything, and although I am sure she didn't want to ask or pressure me, she would very politely ask if I was going to be able to give her anything. All she eventually wanted was enough to pay a bill here or there. She kept on working to the very end.

Although I couldn't pay much to my mother, I think she gained something money can't buy. There might have come a feeling of purpose—a small sense of fulfillment from the use of her God-given talents and something to look forward to each day after retiring and aging. I am sure she enjoyed talking to all kinds of different people every day. Having people to talk and laugh with is very important to a person who is a loner, doesn't have many friends, and didn't think they were well liked. Oftentimes those phone calls became more than a business conversation.

They became chitchat or an opportunity to give advice or just an opportunity to laugh out loud. I also believe that doing all the things she was doing made her feel important. It gave her a sense of pride, made her realize that she had God-given mental abilities. As a side note, I believe one of the things that is harmful and detrimental is that people are made to seem useless as they age. We too often treat them as if they have nothing to offer. What a shame. We waste all this untapped wisdom and knowledge and expertise all because we are prejudiced against the aged. My mother continued to serve RA Educational Services into her eighties and nineties. Sure, I felt the need from time to time to question something she did or indicate that I wanted something done differently. Sure, her mental abilities began to wear down a bit. I am sure she was getting tired keeping track of money, taking calls for new customers, handling complaints, and on and on.

Unfortunately, as I write this book, the company is all but gone, and Mom is no longer taking calls or keeping records. From the time the company was in full swing, I am glad it was something that gave meaning and purpose to her life. I am glad there came a time when she was able to quit her housekeeping job. She was very frugal and somehow made it off of a small amount of social security, the little I was able to give her and some tax return she was able to claim each year. I wish I could tell her one more time, "Thank you, Mom, for your years of service."

For young people their joy is the children God gives them. For older people it can probably be said that the grandchildren and great grandchildren are their joy. They are young people to be around and to spoil. The faces above are grandchildren and great grandchildren she lived to see. Perhaps one of her regrets is that she didn't have the financial resources to spoil them as she wanted to.

Chapter 21
MOM, I WANT TO MAKE YOU HAPPY

W e often shy away from the thought that we can bring a certain amount of joy or happiness into someone's life, even if it is only temporal. We may be prone to believe it is out of the question to even contemplate the notion we can bring a ray of sunshine into the midst of gathering clouds. To escape the challenge of bringing about that joy or happiness, it becomes easier to simply lay the fault at the door of the person suffering. On the other hand, we oftentimes want the benefits of others to bring about that same joy or happiness into our lives.

I have surrendered my life to my Lord and Savior, Jesus Christ. I believe the Bible is the Word of God and that it is the source of all truth. I therefore believe that true peace, joy, happiness, and contentment comes ultimately from God. I would like to quote a couple of biblical texts. In Nehemiah, chapter 8 verse 10 (NKJV), we will find these words: "For the joy of the Lord is your strength." In the book of Isaiah, chapter 26 verse 3 (KJV), we read, "Thou will keep him in perfect peace, whose mind is stayed on thee because he trusteth in thee." In Matthew, chapter

11 verse 28 (NKJV), we read, "Come to Me, all you who labor and are heavy laden, and I will give you rest."

There is a side of us that God has given us that wants to see people happy. It is called compassion. We don't want to see people in pain, unhappy, miserable, and generally melancholy if we can intervene. My dear mother had what I believe was a pretty difficult life. There were some things involving my mom's life that there is no need to talk about here and others that I have already mentioned in previous chapters. I loved her and constantly wanted to do anything that would make her life happy. I wanted her to experience things she had never experienced. I wanted the burden to be lifted and the cloud to be removed. Ultimately, I realized that the burden and the cloud could only entirely be removed when the healer himself would reach down and apply salve to the scars.

My mind from the time I was a little kid until a man in his sixties was always contemplating on how I could be a blessing to my mother. Earlier in this book, I mentioned how I would go out and look for apples on the neighbor's tree to bring home to have them cooked for breakfast. To this day, I still remember going out early in the morning to collect soda bottles, redeeming them and purchasing a variety pack of cereal. I had such a happy heart being able to bring that cereal home, setting it on the table, and my sister Carolyn and I getting to choose a box of cereal. As I got a little older and made a little more money by carrying people's groceries to their cars from the stores or having a paper route, I got great enjoyment from being able to buy my mom presents on Valentine's Day, Mother's Day, Christmas, and her birthday. Who doesn't remember that five-dollar bottle of perfume or that heart-shaped box of chocolates?

As I grew older and made more money, my mom's to-do list became a little more ambitious. One project comes to mind. I believe I was a senior in high school. The house we lived in was a nice house, with a small backyard and front yard. The backyard was about fifteen feet by twenty feet of just grass. The yard was part hill and part flat area. The flat area was about fifteen feet by ten feet. Well, it was my idea—not sure it was a good one—to dig up this section of it and build a concrete patio. This was an ambitious project. The yard needed to be dug up with a shovel, framed out, reinforced with wire, then we had to construct a chute so that concrete could be transported from the top of our hill down to the bottom, where the patio would be. Not only that but I had to make arrangements to get the concrete. All this had to be done by a nineteen-year-old with no money, no experience, and only one friend to help pour the concrete. I am sure the neighbors who knew what was going on thought, *What in the world is that boy doing*? I wanted my mom to have a patio. Sometimes our heart can get in the way of good judgment. That patio got poured, but it was not of professional quality. I was no concrete finisher. To be honest, I can't say my mom was overjoyed with the results. I really don't remember her saying much, but she didn't criticize me either. I am assuming that in her heart she was pleased her son had made the effort even though it wasn't high quality. It has been over forty years, and that patio is still there even though the top layer has deteriorated pretty badly and needs to be replaced.

There were other ambitious projects I took on just to be a blessing to my mom. I reframed our basement so that there would be a private washroom and a little back room and an enclosed room for the furnace and water heater. I paneled the walls, and boy, we were going to have the best basement in the neighborhood. Again, I must confess that this high school boy did not have professional carpentry skills. That basement stayed about 75 percent complete up until my fifties. It only got a professional job because somehow when my mom was in her late eighties or early nineties the basement was flooded, and the insurance company paid for it to be renovated. Ms. Anderson finally got a quality basement late in life even though she wasn't able to go up and down the steps to enjoy it.

Although my carpentry and concrete skills left a lot to be desired, I meant well. One thing I did fairly well was landscaping. I loved digging up Mom's yard and replanting it with flowers where there was grass. Every year I was adding more plants or sprucing up the other parts of the yard. She had what I think was one of the nicer-looking yards on our block, if not the nicest looking. Mom also loved the yard. To this day, I don't understand what coffee grounds and eggshells have to do with plant growth, but for all the years I can remember she would take her coffee grounds and eggshells and gently spread them around the plants.

Catherine Anderson never really got to go places. It was basically work and stay home, with the exception of the times she got to go with my sister out shopping or to dinner at Carolyn's or sometimes if her granddaughter had an event, but that was the extent of her escapades. Mom was a loner, and she didn't keep in contact with her extended family. As I grew older, I was quite aware she rarely went anywhere, so as part of trying to bring some joy or happiness her way I was always planning little one-day trips or weekend trips for her. I was always excited about going to places like Atlanta Georgia or Niagara Falls Canada or New York, Philadelphia, and Williamsburg, Virginia. Although many of these family trips were not as nice as they could be, because somehow a squabble would come uninvited, I was still determined that Mom was going to see some places she had never been and would be happy. I need to say a little something about my wife here. My wife, Frances, is as humble and patient as one can be. She was always a willing participant in my plans for my mother. No matter where I planned to go, she never argued or threw cold water on it. She just wanted me to slow down a little, as I was aging right along with my mother.

Anywhere I could take Catherine Anderson, I would. Church events, out to breakfast, out to dinner, to visit friends, drives on a nice day. In the back of my mind, there was always a plan to take her somewhere or to do something for her. I tried hard to make her happy. Ultimately, only God can really make any of us truly happy, but it still feels good to care for and be thoughtful about another person's existence, especially if that person is Mom.

I am an adventurer by nature. As it turns out .my mother is too. In the top picture I took her up to the beautiful Appalachian Mountains off of Skyline drive in Front Royal Virginia. This outing took place in the 1970s. The bottom picture shows mom mounted on a horse preparing for a light jaunt along a trail somewhere in West Virginia. To my knowledge this is probably our mother's first experience horseback riding.

I was able to take my mother to historic Williamsburg Va. I believe that to be a replica of a 19th century cabin in the background. The bottom picture is of us at Niagara Falls Canada.

Top picture: Mom and I standing in front of the new Martin Luther King statue in Washington D.C. Unfortunately the head of the statue did not get included in the picture. Our mother was in either her late eighties or early nineties. In the bottom picture we are standing in front of the Spirit of Washington boat preparing to take a luncheon cruise down the Potomac River. Mom was probably in her early nineties.

Out on a 2 hour luncheon cruise down the Potomac Rive aboard the Spirit of Washington. An official of the ship graciously consents to take a picture with my mom. I am sure it made her feel a little special.

Me and my beloved mother pose while sitting on a bench at the beautiful Oronoco Park in beautiful Alexandria Virginia.

Chapter 22
THE ACCIDENT

A s our mother begin to age, I felt a need to go over a little more often and take her out to breakfast or lunch. I just wanted her to get out and about. I relished the opportunity to spend time with her. I was fortunate that although she was right at ninety or a little over, she was in fairly good health. Her pace had slowed, but she really didn't need much assistance. She was still living by herself in the three-level house and was quite able to go up and down the stairs several times a day. She was so independent that it rarely ever crossed my mind that she would slip and fall at home. I had to remind myself whenever I called, and she didn't answer the phone right away, that it was just taking her longer to get there.

On a beautiful morning in June 2015, I went over to pick her up for breafast and then off to purchase a pair of reading glasses. We went to a McDonald's in the DC metropolitan area. I don't remember, but I am pretty sure Mom had coffee—if nothing else, she wanted her coffee—pancakes, and sausage. I probably had the same thing. We sat down, talked a little, ate, and left. From there we drove over to a well-known chain store to purchase the glasses. I doubt seriously if she would entertain the idea of waiting in the car while

I went in. I think I know my mother well enough to say with confidence that she would want to go in to make sure she picked out those glasses.so I really don't think there was any discussion about her taking that walk from the parking lot up to and into the store. Once inside this fairly large store, I had the task of finding out where the glasses where displayed. I spotted an employee, who might have been a manager, and he proceeded to walk me to the location of the glasses. While walking with the employee, my ninety something-year-old mom was walking behind us, trying to keep up. Of course, I wasn't thinking and should have been aware that she was not thirty years old, and I needed to walk beside her. My mind was so focused on the glasses that I just lost track of her. Within a few minutes, for some reason I turned around. I either heard a thump or just instinctively turned to see how she was doing. At any rate, when I turned around, I was stunned to see my precious mother sprawled out on the floor. She had fallen. While no one can prove how she fell, I believe she tripped on an in-floor grate.

Again, I was not thinking clearly. I should have realized there was a strong possibility she had fractured or broken a bone. To me, Mom was strong, in good health, probably going to live to be a hundred. We just needed to get her up on her feet and take her home. How silly! No, she wasn't going home. We were able to get her up into to a wheelchair, and we called an ambulance. The manager of the store wasn't very compassionate or helpful. I believe if there was a way to get my mother to the car and home, he would have gone along with it. He probably didn't want to deal with an elderly lady getting hurt on this store's property while he was the manager on duty. Of course, I don't know that for sure—it is just a suspicion on my part. Mom was in a lot of pain but did not complain or demonstrate it. She didn't blame me. She didn't blame the store. She could have done either one.

Within about fifteen minutes, the ambulance was there and after answering some questions she was off to the hospital. Not long after arriving at the hospital, tests were done, and the doctor consulted with us, and the news was not good. My mom was so durable, so strong, that I just knew it would be some type of bruise and a couple of days' rest, and she would be on her way. No, that wasn't the case. There was a fracture somewhere in her hip. Just about every adult knows that a hip fracture or a fracture in that area is very bad news, especially for someone my mother's age. I don't really remember how I reacted to the news. I feel pretty sure I was devastated and fearful. I am sure I blamed myself. After all, I should have kept an eye on her. She was an elderly woman. How could I expect her to keep up with me and the store clerk? I was frightened by the thought of her getting anesthesia and then being under the knife for a couple of hours. I just didn't know if she would make it. It is amazing that sometimes as Christians, in a time of crisis or challenge, we fall apart. We have stored in our minds years of scriptural promises we have heard or memorized. We are sometimes prone to give others advice in their times of crisis. Often, we have heard a very powerful biblical message that says we can conquer the world. We say, "Yeah! Bring it on! I am ready." Then we fall apart in the moment. Faith becomes doubt, and our roar becomes a whimper.

God is merciful. I don't know how I would have lived with myself if that surgery had ended in my mom's death. Death may sound a little drastic to consider but considering my mom's age, the thought I am sure crossed my mind. The surgery went well. She came through with flying colors, and now it was all about healing and recovery. I was extremely grateful to God and the doctor. I felt very confident that within a few months she would be back up on her feet. The plan was for her to stay in the hospital a couple of days and then go to a nursing home for recovery. Of course, that recovery would include lots of physical and mental therapy. The goal was to get her to the point that she could do everything she did prior to her injury.

The nursing home was not the best experience for my mom. It was a cultural shock. She was this healthy, independent woman. She had in the last few years of her life been spending lots of money at co-op and health food stores, buying all the right types of food, vitamins, and supplements. Although she had very little money, her reasoning was that she would sacrifice if it kept her out of the doctor's office. She was constantly getting very good reports from her doctor after each routine visit. She lived by herself, and she could climb up and down the stairs with ease. She was taking care of herself, doing both inside and outside chores. She probably never envisioned herself in a nursing home, but there she was.

Over the next month or two, I was a daily visitor at the nursing home. She loved her coffee, so I would stop at McDonald's and get a hot cup of coffee. Sometimes I would bring her other things to eat. She really did not like the nursing home food and based on what I could discern she did not eat much. She was already a slight woman of barely one hundred pounds, and not eating could be dangerous. So, it was incumbent on me and others to bring something from the outside world from time to time.

Mom was diligent about her therapy. Her can-do attitude, her persistence paid dividends. She excelled—for someone her age— in all the physical and mental exercises they gave her. It finally came to the point she had completed everything asked of her. She was ready to go home. There was some angst about her going home with the understanding that she would be staying alone. My mother was not going to leave her home under any circumstances, and she valued her privacy. My wife and I could have moved in, but then our privacy would be gone—the house was very small. I guess if Mom would not have been able to make it, then we would just have had to move in with her. She would not have wanted to come and live with us. I have a lovely, loving, giving wife who would have said okay to us moving in with my mother, even if it meant cramped quarters and no privacy, but that would not have been fair to Frances.

Amazingly, and by the mercy of God, we only needed to stay with her a couple of days, and she was able to do pretty much everything she did prior to her surgery. No, I wasn't comfortable with her being alone after hip surgery and living in a three-story house, where she would be going up and down the stairs, but my comfort level grew as time went on.

Some readers might be wondering if there were any lawsuits filed on behalf of Catherine Anderson. To start with, we tried very hard to find a lawyer to take our case, but none would do so on a pro bono arrangement. They just concluded that there was no clear-cut victory. This particular store chain was just too powerful, and the law was on their side. I appealed to the store. We took pictures of where the fall took place, but there was nothing that could be done. The store clearly took the position that it was my mom's fault. I was saddened that I had to tell her this bad news. With her God-given strong intestinal fortitude, she moved on, although deep inside I knew she thought, *Story of my life.*

Every woman wants to look beautiful. Part of the plan is to make regular visits to the beautician. Our mother was no different except she had to be very frugal and so couldn't enjoy those regular visits. Her children came first. She managed to be her own beautician for many. many years. As the years went on I just assume my mother had no interest in going to the beautician. At one point I was able to convince her to go. The appointment was made with Nat the Beautician. Carolyn the older sister picked her up and off they went. Our beloved mother in her nineties above looks fabulous.

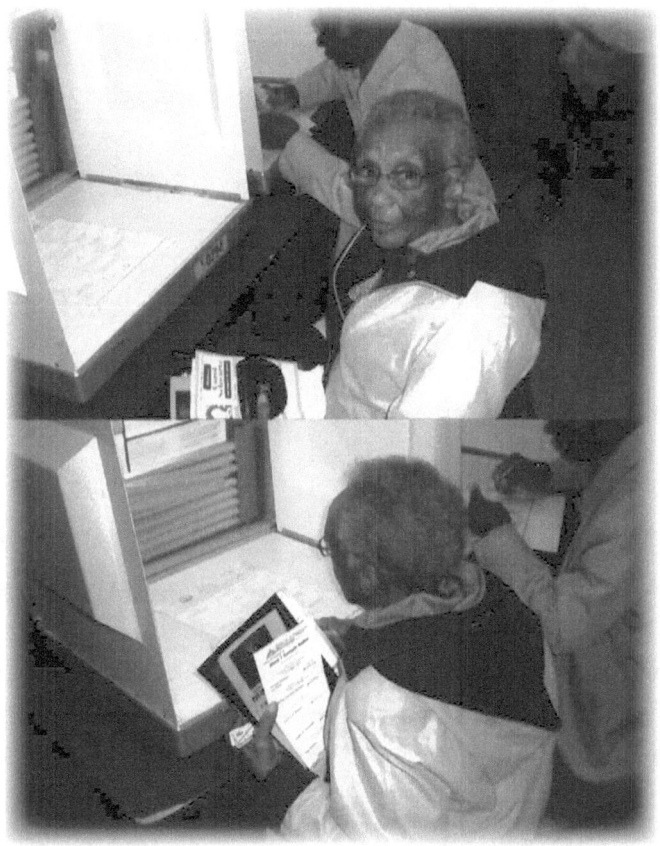

In the year 2008 roughly one hundred thirty million people made the decision to vote in the presidential election featuring the first African American candidate to head a major presidential party ticket. On Tuesday November 4th,2008 I drove to 4207 Hst. to pick up my 87 year old mother and drive her a few blocks away to her voting precinct. Once at Davis Elementary School I escorted this elderly woman inside the school where they graciously seated her and handed her pencil and paper ballot. After carefully looking over the ballot she became one of approximately seventy million people to vote for Mr. Barack Hussein Obama who became our 44th president of these United States. What a proud moment for our beloved mother.

Chapter 23
MOM IS AGING

Everyone ages. That's no surprise. Adam's fall in the Garden of Eden assures us that we will age, and we will die. It is the "curse." We may try to deny it with hair coloring, facial creams, youthful clothing, surgery, etc. No matter what we do, we are all aging. The body grows tired, the shoulders droop, the knees hurt, the back aches, and the skin sags. Our steps are shorter, and so it takes us longer to get from point A to point B. Of course, while we ourselves are aging, we are watching those around us age. Our neighbors who we have known over the years are noticeably older and begin to either die, move away into nursing homes, or move in with relatives. We can't believe how worn out our childhood television and movie stars look as they enter their seventies and eighties. What about our childhood athletes? We can't believe they are the same ones who were so vivacious, so energetic, so seemingly indestructible. What about our childhood friends? We catch up to each other when we hit our sixties, and we can't believe it is the same person with whom we grew up. Joe has a potbelly, gray hair, wrinkles all over, and a cane. We try to be polite and say how well he looks, and he hasn't changed at all, but we know this is a lie.

Then there is Mom and Dad. As kids, we thought they would live forever. We expected to see them every day after school, or as we grew older, after work. We knew we would always spend Christmas and Thanksgiving with them. Even after we moved away from home, we expected every time we called that they would answer the phone. Every time we would go visit they would answer the door. We knew they would be at our weddings and some day in the future spend time with their grandchildren. Years go by, and then one day it grabs us. There is the gray hair; the slow walk; the fiftieth, sixtieth, or seventieth birthday; and we realize that aging has set in. We might try to deny it, but we are forced into reality. We are forced to have those conversations about wills, location of insurance policy, funeral arrangements, and desires. Nobody wants to talk about it, but we know we must start that dreaded conversation. We are forced to think and talk about things like alternative living arrangements and the very strong possibility that life for our loved ones is coming to an end. I am not sure exactly when my mother's mortality hit me, but somewhere during her eighties and nineties it became a continuous thought about how much time Catherine Anderson might have left on this earth. Her pending demise had a greater hold on me after her hip injury and surgery. One of my greatest desires and unspoken requests to God was that Mom would live to be a hundred and beyond. This was not a pipe dream. She was fairly healthy and of sound mind, and she was still able to live alone and take care of herself. She was climbing stairs, cooking her meals, keeping track of her doctors' appointments, and paying bills. She was still an efficient secretary. She was taking calls, assigning tutors, and keeping track of payments. Her mind was still very much intact into her eighties and early nineties. The one thing she couldn't do was go into the basement and wash clothes. I would gather her clothes together every week or two and take them downstairs and wash them and dry them. I am sure she was discouraged that she couldn't do this small act anymore. Mom was very independent, and had been all her life, but she was a woman of common sense, and she wasn't going to risk falling down the steps and having another hip injury.

Even though she was rapidly aging, we still tried to do things together. On some birthdays, I would try to put on an informal birthday party. It wasn't a surprise. We would have ten to fifteen people over, light up the candles, sing "Happy Birthday," and have small talk. I believe we celebrated Mom's ninetieth birthday which may have been our last in house birthday party. She was frail, and her cognitive abilities were waning. The small living room was crowded. Nothing special, but we were just trying to say, "Mom, you are special," which was the goal at each of these birthday parties. To be honest, I doubt if my mom ever had a birthday cake growing up. I doubt she ever had people sing "Happy Birthday" or give her a present growing up. If I had the opportunity, I would have liked to have thrown a big, elegant party for her one hundredth birthday. Pull out all the stops. Spare no expense.

After her hip surgery, I knew Frances and I needed to spend even more time with her. It occurred to me that Sunday evenings would be a good time to spend with her. My loving wife was willing to do whatever it took to make Mom's life comfortable. For example, on Sundays we would go over, and Frances would cook a very nice dinner that we would all sit down and enjoy together. After dinner we would wash the dishes and thoroughly clean the kitchen and dining area. On days when the weather was nice, we would pack the dinner and go to a nice park somewhere and eat at a picnic table. The last time we were able to eat at a park came when we took some ice cream and cake and headed for a nice place outside. It was a beautiful day. The sun was shining- a simply gorgeous day. It was a lovely day to get Mom out to soak up the rays. We went to a park near an area where she grew up. We sat and enjoyed the ice cream. Mom gazed around at the children playing and the dogs running around. Walking back to the car, she walked very slowly, stumbling along the way. She was barely able to keep her balance. I am trying not to pay attention to the slow pace, or unsteadiness, knowing they are the steps of decline, perhaps even impending death. Our car was parked in front of what had been an old school building. We surmised that it may have been a school that she attended as a little kid.

As we drove away from the area, we passed through my mom's old neighborhood. I pointed out the church she attended as a kid. There was the house at 515 E Street that belonged to some of her siblings. Then we also saw the house that she grew up in as a kid. This obviously had an effect on her, as the next day she was excitedly telling people that I "took her on vacation." Mom was declining mentally. To her, that little two- or three-minute drive through her neighborhood was a vacation. Who knows? That imaginary vacation she went on might have been the best in her life. I am glad we got to go. It would be our last.

Chapter 24
JESUS, HELP US!

F or anyone who has ever been in a desperate, dire situation, they know these tragic events come out of the blue and strip us of our sense of control. Believers in the Almighty know that unless he intervenes this is not going to end well. If a person doesn't believe in God, perhaps at that moment of desperation they will hope they are wrong, and if they are alone, they might utter words like, "God, if you are there, please help." Well, I believe in the Almighty, all-sufficient God, and never did I feel so helpless and in need of his intervention than on that day in April 2017, when I went to visit my dear, beloved mother.

A hip injury, surgery, and aging had taken its toll on our mother, along with the stress of keeping the creditors at bay and being concerned for her children and grandchildren. I am sure every day felt like an uphill journey. Her appetite had started to dwindle. All she appeared to have an appetite for was a cup of coffee and some kind of sugary snack. Her loss of appetite became my battle. Everyday either for breakfast, lunch, or dinner I would go over and try to fix a meal. I admit I was a bit scheming and tricky—maybe we call it untruthful or lying—to get her to eat. I had to tell her many times that I wanted to eat with her even though I really wasn't hungry. I just fabricated something, knowing she wouldn't turn my invitation to eat with her.

On this particular day, I went over for breakfast. I remember I fixed her a sausage patty and a scrambled egg, and she had a cup of coffee. I did not have anything to eat that morning. I just sat in a chair across from her, and we started to chitchat. The next thing I knew, my mother's cup of coffee had spilled over on the table, and I remember saying something like, "Oh, Mama, you spilled your coffee." I got up to get some paper towels about two feet away, and when I turned to wipe the table, I knew that was not an accidental spill. My mind became frozen in time as I saw my precious mother sliding down the chair. Over the next few seconds, my confused mind tried to process what was taking place. To my horror, I thought she was having a massive heart attack. Later I understood she wasn't having a heart attack; she was having a stroke. As I went over to her, I could see her stomach was staring to swell, so I started pushing in an upward direction on her abdomen, trying to bring up anything that was not allowing her to breathe properly. Thank you God some food came up. I didn't know what else physically to do. I thought our beloved mother was going to die right in front of me. I am a Christian and I personally believe Jesus Christ is God the Son. I believe in a personal God who hears and answers the prayers of His children. I believe that as a matter of protocol we should always call out to God -in the name of Jesus-first, in time of calamity. I do understand that not everyone reading this book will hold the same theological belief but it is my position. Overwhelmed in the moment, I said in a very firm voice, "Mama, call on Jesus". So there we were the both of us- me imploring Jesus outwardly to help us and perhaps silently my mom doing the same. I called 911 in a panic, and by the grace of God the ambulance was there within ten minutes. As I said in an earlier part of this book I remember becoming upset with the 911 operator because she kept asking all these questions that in my mind I thought were a waste of time. As I was to find out later, the ambulance had already been dispatched while they were still asking questions. Those questions were important and was vital information that could be passed onto the medics as they drove towards their destination. After the call I am not quite sure about the order of other events, but I think I called my wife next and frantically told her to pray. I called my sister in Missouri and my other sister in Waldorf, Maryland. As I think about it, I probably terrified my poor mother as I became so full of panic.

In a very short time the ambulance was there and my mom appeared to have stabilized to the point where she was sitting up in the chair by herself. I was able to leave her momentarily while I went to answer the door for the medics. They asked a few questions and positioned my mom into a chair, not a stretcher. They must have determined quickly that this was a stroke and not a heart attack. It was all so surreal. We just never know what a day holds. I expected to go see Mom, fix some breakfast, talk a little, and be on my way, but within thirty minutes or so my mom was in the back of an ambulance, with the medic attending to her, sirens blasting, and us on our way to the hospital. No sound came out of my mom's mouth. Complete silence. I am sure she was very scared, not fully understanding what had happened or what the near future held for her. All I truly remember about the ride to the hospital is that we ran into a funeral, and the driver became frustrated, as he probably figured we were rushing against time. Even though I didn't know where we were going and couldn't see anything, I had complete confidence that the driver would get us there. I also remember the sadness that began to well up inside me as the tears started to come. Out of all things, I started a conversation with the medic attending to my mother about his own mother. I just needed someone to understand.

Within about ten minutes, we were pulling up to Providence Hospital in Washington, DC. When they got her out of the ambulance, I graciously thanked them and went in to be with her. As a side note, whenever I tell the story about the stroke, people tell me how blessed I am that my mother didn't have her stroke alone. I could have not come that day or got there a little later or left a little early, and she would have laid on the floor, terrified, and maybe died. She never told me, but I am sure she felt a little comfort or peace because I was there. Not that I could have made the outcome different, but people need the presence of others in the midst of their crisis.

It wasn't long before my sister Carolyn was there and later her daughter Erika—Catherine's eldest granddaughter. While the doctors in the emergency room worked on our mother, Carolyn and I waited in another area. Before long Carolyn broke down crying. That was her mother lying on that bed, having suffered a massive stroke. I know she was crying because of love and maybe crying because she knew all the pain her mother had gone through in her life. The good news for us was that the doctors were able to administer some type of anti stroke medicine, which I guess was designed to slow down the destruction. Unfortunately, as we later found out, the damage had already been done.

Chapter 25
CONTINUING
THE JOURNEY

G od is so gracious and kind to the United States. One of the ways that his kindness shows up is in our understanding of illnesses. We have garnered so much information about various diseases. We have so much insight and can plan out a strategy to attack almost any illness. Granted, we can't cure every illness, but we can at least have a comfortable level of hope under almost any circumstances. Think of how far we have come in just the last fifty years. Organ transplants are almost as common as dental surgery. Cancer, diabetes, and other dreaded diseases are often controlled or outright cured. In the past, these sicknesses were a death sentence. The hope that modern medicine has given us has skyrocketed. This is the graciousness of our God. Something else that might go overlooked is that God has put it into the hearts of our doctors that people of old age require and should receive the same amount of care that a young person with perhaps fifty years of life ahead of them. If an elderly person has stage four cancer, there is no reason to assume he or she will be sent home to die, with no attempt at saving his or her life.

On the day my mother entered Providence Hospital as a ninety-six-year-old with a massive stroke, they went right to work on her. Never once did I get the impression, they thought she was too old to try and save. No, once they stabilized her, they realized she needed to be in a hospital more equipped to deal with her stroke. Within a matter of a couple of hours, they made arrangements to send her to Washington Hospital Center. This particular hospital was more equipped to deal with strokes. They had specialized personnel and equipment. So, onto the stretcher, into the ambulance, and off to Washington Hospital Center, about fifteen minutes away. It was going to be a long night for all of us. My poor mom must have felt truly frightened. She probably wondered where her family was. Were we just outside, or had we gone home? How horrible it must be for anyone, especially an older person, to be alone in the midst of something like a stroke. Of course, the stroke had taken away her speech, so we couldn't communicate with her and determine what her actual fears were. I remember on the way over to the hospital she had taken hold of some kind of wire or tubing and was twisting it as if to calm her nerves. It also seemed that she stared aimlessly between the wire she was twisting and the ceiling of the ambulance. Endless thoughts were no doubt racing through her mind. Perhaps she also was whispering prayers to God who could help her during this very uncertain and frightful ordeal.

Once inside the hospital in a temporary room, there was a lot of going and coming between doctors, nurses, therapists, and other staff. The whole idea was to ascertain the extent of the damage. I broke down emotionally. Was our dear mother here because I had misunderstood the doctor, whom I thought to have heard him say she didn't need certain medicines anymore? Did I misunderstand her need to take or not take the thyroid medicine anymore? Did I do something wrong? I was beginning to blame myself. Even though I had not been careless I felt the weight of her situation bearing down on me. Our mother was seeing several doctors and was taking several different medications. Honestly, my mother kept up with her medicine better than I did. She had a keen mind and was always letting me know when something was running low or had run out. To this day, I sometimes think if I had done something different she would not have had that stroke. While I admit that thought is very rare now, some four years later, even now as I write this book it has come to my mind. On that first evening at Washington Hospital Center, I had a breaking moment. The tears flowed as I contemplated the thought that my mother was there because I had mismanaged the medicine. Thankfully, there was a doctor there with whom I shared my concerns. He made me understand that I did nothing wrong. There is a multitude of reasons as to why someone could have such a catastrophic stroke, like my mom. Of course her age might have been a major contributor along with the constant stress she lived under. Ultimately only God knows what brought on the stroke. We leave that unknown with Him.

Mom was paralyzed on her right side. She couldn't swallow or talk. She still had blood on the brain from the broken vessel. At her age, it was too dangerous to do any surgery. The only thing to do was wait and see if some parts of her body would rebound and come back to use. Apparently, if that was going to happen, it would show signs in a few days. For now, they had to devise a way to make sure they could get food into her body. Her age made it unwise to do a surgery that would connect a feeding tube into her abdomen. The only thing to do was insert a feeding tube down through her nose into the stomach and feed her that way. From day one, she made it known she didn't like it, and it wasn't going to work. I remember her yanking at the tube in order to pull it out after they tried inserting it. In some way, I guess that was a good sign, as even after a major stroke she was still spicy. On the other hand, she had to eat, and as I found out in the days ahead the hope would be that she could somehow train herself to swallow very small portions of soft food such as applesauce. This was going to be a tremendous task and also a risky one as she good very easy choke in a manner that could bring on further damage-even death. Perhaps the next surreal event for me was when in her room I saw the heart monitor speed up, and Mom started fighting as if she was terrified she was going to die at any moment. If I remember correctly, the monitor was reading in the range of 160 bpm. I guess it should have been obvious, but it really dawned on me that the reading simply meant her heart was beating at 160 beats per minute. That rapid heart rate was something our mother sensed, which probably explains why she demonstrated some fear. If a person's heart starts racing while they are resting, fear would almost certainly come over them. The doctor who was attending to her pulled me over to a vacant room. He said it was possible our mother could die at any minute. Reading between the lines, I assume he was saying her heart couldn't continue to beat at that pace. He advised we not agree to have her resuscitated, as she was so small that any compression on the chest area would crush her. At this moment my Christian instincts arose, and to the doctor's surprise—I am sure—I asked him if I could pray for him. I wanted God to give him all the wisdom necessary to take care of our mother. God heard this man's cry of desperation, and by his grace the doctors were able to give Mom some medication that slowed her heart rate. We were all extremely grateful and were able to leave that hospital that night with a sigh of relief.

Over the next few days, I would make the trek up to the hospital, most of the time just me and my thoughts and a word of prayer to God. My mother had lost almost all her ability to swallow, so she was getting very little to eat. The nurse would have to prepare food a certain way and hope she would be able to get a couple spoonfuls down her throat without choking and perhaps suffocating her to death. Of course, Mom was not the only patient, and the nurse couldn't spend hours on end trying to feed her, so she spent maybe fifteen minutes tops—I don't really remember. I would come with my slice of lemon meringue pie, maybe some warm oatmeal, and a cup of coffee. I would have to put some thickener into the coffee, and off we went. The thickener was needed to keep her from taking anything liquid that would possibly go down into her lungs. Small positive signs could make me giddy. I remember once when she ate what I believed to be half a slice of pie, and I went away almost floating on air. I really believe she was fighting to make it. On the other hand I am sure she had a desire to give up as bouts of depression and weariness would set in when things started to go in a negative direction. When I talk about depression and weariness setting in, it should be understood that I also had to deal with and with God's help fight off these two destroyers.. Perhaps at this point she had become drained of the will to live. Life is like that. Some days we are determined to fight, and then there are days when we just want to give up. May God, in his mercy, help us all not give up.

I was pumped with excitement by any sign of improvement. At one point I called my sister Pam from the cell phone and put it up to mom's ear. When Pam said something, my mother almost snapped her vocal cords trying to respond. She was so thrilled to hear Pam's voice. She made a sound, but it was unintelligible. Then came the moment when they were able to take her out of bed and set her up in a chair. She had to be strapped in because her body was unable to sustain an upright posture, but what a joy to see her sitting up. Next came the physical therapist, a bubbly young girl with a lot of enthusiasm. I watched as she worked with her, trying to get her to sit up in the bed on her own. I was very upbeat with the kindness of this young girl and just knew that with her help my mother was going to be on her way to recovery. It wasn't long before all my enthusiasm came to a screeching halt as we got the dreaded request for a family meeting. The proverbial bubble busted. I did not know much about these family meetings, but I assumed they were to notify families that things were not looking good for the patient. The time and date were scheduled, and it came. In attendance were my sister Carolyn; my wife, Frances; Carolyn's husband, Johnny; Carolyn's daughter Erika; and my sister Pam by phone. I believe there were three doctors and a counselor also there. All the doctors and counselor made their remarks, but it basically came down to, "I am sorry, but your mother is not going to live." Those might not be the exact words, but it was the essence.

If I remember correctly, they even stated she didn't have long to live. The tears came freely from my eyes, as I couldn't believe what I was hearing and really did not want to accept what was being said. I asked questions, but I really wanted to say, "No, my mother will live." Those doctors took no pleasure in saying our mother would die. I know they did all they could and did not come to that conclusion in a cavalier way. They were very kind, and to this day I am very appreciative for all they did but I was not going to endorse a death sentence for my mom. In my mind, no matter what the doctors said, I held on to the hope that God was going to heal Catherine Anderson. I remember even telling this to a counselor, who was very nice. I wanted those doctors to know that God could override science. I wanted them to not be so dogmatic about pronouncing a death sentence. I wanted a different outcome for my mother so those doctors would be encouraged to say to others whose loved ones are dying, "We have done all we can, and although we believe this person is going to die, God can intervene." Yes I wanted them to be able for them to give others a hope beyond science.

I guess the next downer was when we were notified that our mother was being released from the hospital and sent to a nursing home. I knew she wouldn't get the same medical care at a nursing home as at a hospital, especially a good hospital as I believed we were at. I wanted her to stay there under the care of the professionals, hoping and believing she was going to be one of those miracle cases, but it wasn't to be. My contact was now not so much with the doctors as it was with the social worker. It would be just a matter of days before my mom's frail body was laid on a stretcher and driven to the nursing home that had an available bed. I was hoping for a delay, but a nursing home became readily available, and the next phase of our lives began.

Chapter 26
THE NURSING HOME

I n chapter 1 of this book, I talked about awful days—
days which God, in his love, only allows us to experience
a few of in our lifetime. These are days marked by some
overwhelming, horrific event that rocks our world and shakes
us to our knees. It's a time of seeming hopelessness, a time when
everything seems dark. It hits us out of nowhere, like a bolt of
lightning. In chapter 25, I had another one of those awful days.
It was the dreaded family meeting requested by the hospital.
They had done everything they could. It had come time for
them to do the right thing. They had to tell us it didn't seem
likely my mother was going to live. I remember how freely the
tears flowed. All the questions I asked led back to the same
conclusion: they had done all they could do, and she would not
live long-perhaps that meant only a few weeks or months, The
next thing would be to get her to a nursing home where she
could still receive the professional care she needed while living
out her final days. My mom's future was now in the hands of the
social workers, who would do their best to find a suitable nursing
facility. In my heart, I was hoping they wouldn't be able to find
one, or at least it would take a few weeks. I was still hopeful and
confident that Mom would get better, and she needed to be in

the hospital to get maximum care. I am sure if those doctors thought they could do more they would have done it. This was a ninety-six-year-old woman who had suffered a massive stroke. There was really nothing more they could do. My task was to be grateful to God for each new day he gave us. I had to see that every day I had my mother was a victory. Every day I drove to the hospital and peeked my head in the open door of her room and saw Catherine Anderson lying in bed was a great relief.

The weeks I had hoped for her to stay at the hospital became only a matter of days. The day of departure came. They made arrangements to have my frail mother gingerly placed on a stretcher, placed in the back of the ambulance, and driven through the busy streets of DC and on to the highway to a nursing home in Prince George's County, Maryland. I can only imagine the thoughts that were swirling through her mind as she drove to her next stop of hopeful treatment. Then again, maybe there were no thoughts, just a dark cloud hanging over her in the quietness of her soul. If I had to guess, I would think she had come to a point of resignation—*I am never going to see 4207 H Street again. I am not going to live.*

I don't know the exact date that we got her registered, but I do remember it was right around Mother's Day. It was probably around the middle of the week, with Mother's Day being that Sunday. That Mother's Day felt a little awkward for me. I felt as though I should spend the entire day at the nursing home with my mom, but on the other hand, I needed to help Frances have an enjoyable day. As it turned out, God gave us a beautiful day. I got to take Frances out to dinner and then we came over to spend time with Mom. On this Mother's Day, these two ladies and a man came to my mom's room and gave her a beautiful plant. These two kind ladies had mothers in the home, and they had made it their mission to be a blessing and advocate for the other patients on the floor. One of the ladies, whose name escapes me, really befriended me. She was like an angel sent to help me. She was a Christian lady who seemed to have taken an interest in my mom and had made herself available for advice, as she was pretty familiar with the ins and outs of this particular nursing home. God, in his kindness, as he will often do, sent someone to help me navigate the entire nursing home experience. Since she was a Christian, she was not only offering me practical advice but spiritual guidance as well. She would visit my mom, and I am sure she prayed for her.

Day after day my routine was the same: get up, get dressed, and head to the nursing home—sometimes once a day, sometimes twice. Mom needed to eat, and nursing home food is not the same as home cooked food., so I would make some oatmeal or take some lemon meringue pie or stop off at KFC and pick up some mashed potatoes and gravy, but I never went without a cup of hot coffee from McDonald's. Not that my mother loved McDonald's coffee. She loved coffee perhaps better than eating, and when she was home, she would make her own fresh-brewed coffee every day. Our beloved mother had already started to lose her appetite prior to the stroke, and now she was barely able to swallow, so she just did not bother to try to eat. I am grateful to the nurses or attendants who would sit with her and try to get her to eat, but it was a daunting task, and I don't doubt they had other patients, so there was only so much time they could spend with her. They may have gotten her to eat a few spoonfuls at a meal. It got to the point that we even considered a few spoonfuls a victory. Even my oatmeal, mashed potatoes, pie, and coffee were not consumed wholeheartedly. I was discouraged but grateful for small victories. I would sometimes ask people who were going to visit if they would perhaps try to get her to eat something. Of course, I had to give very specific instructions on how she was to eat because there was always the possibility of injury or even death from choking. I just hoped she would respond with more effort to people she knew.

One of the things I looked forward to doing was getting Mom up and into her wheelchair—the attendants actually did the work of getting her up and into the chair—and heading onto the elevators and down to the lobby or outside for a stroll and fresh air. While we only could go a couple hundred feet, I dreamed of and prayed for the day when I was going to be able to stroll her over to a nearby shopping center, and we would grab a sandwich at a restaurant. Until then we had to just settle for fifteen to thirty minutes out in the fresh air. This wasn't an easy adventure, as she had a difficult time holding herself up erect, and she would droop. At other times we would sit in the lobby, which was really nicely decorated and very pleasing to the eye, which may in some way have helped take her mind off her sickness. Sometimes, while sitting there, I would feed her. Mom had tried, when asked, to hold her eating utensil in her hand and feed herself. It was very awkward, but again we thank God for small victories. This act of trying to feed herself showed momentary willingness to fight on. One of the things I did cherish about visiting her was the reading of God's Word. The Bible, to me, is not a book of myths and fairy tales. It is the Word of God. In other words, I believe it is the writings of words inspired by God to reveal himself to us and to give us instructions on how to have a personal relationship with him. Apart from praying for my mom and showing her love through practical deeds, there was no greater thing I could do than to keep her before the Lord through his word. Of course, Satan— yes, I believe in a personal devil—and all the demonic beings of hell would have me believe that reading the Word of God was no good.

That it was a waste of time. Nothing could be further from the truth. As Christians, one of the best things we can do is to bring our loved ones into contact with the word of God. Due to her stroke, Satan and the powers of darkness would have had me believe she wouldn't be able to understand it. I am glad I didn't succumb to those thoughts. It is the hearing of God's word that is used to produce faith. In Romans, chapter 10 verse 17 (KJV), we read, "So then faith cometh by hearing, and hearing by the word of God." Always put the Word of God first. By the power of God's Holy Spirit, we will be able to understand it, believe it, and enjoy it. I remember once before my mother was sick and still living at home that I would come by her house once a week, and she would sit down in her comfortable blue chair, and I would sit down in the other chair and read three chapters of scripture beginning from Mathew1:1. I would read without comment, and my mother would sit silently and listen. We did this until we had completed the entire New Testament. My mother didn't give any sign that she enjoyed or appreciated it. It was more like she was just being kind to me, but I have no doubt that spiritual seed was being planted in her.

My routine was pretty much the same when I visited her: Feed Mom, read the Word of God to her, pray with her, and take her out for fresh air or just down to the lobby, not necessarily in that order. When I read the Word of God to her, I would read a variety of things. I would read certain psalms, such as 23, 24, 27, 91 (her favorite), or 103 to help her to rest in God. I would read certain passages that talked about God's power to do miraculous things, such as reverse the damage done by a stroke. I would also and maybe most importantly read scriptures about who Jesus was and how one was to gain salvation by trusting in his finished work on the cross. Thoughts would run through my mind trying to cast doubt concerning her being able to understand great spiritual truths found in books of the Bible, like Romans or Galatians. Dear one, please don't get caught up in trying to figure out if they understand. God is the illuminator of scripture. I thank God for the privilege of reading the Word of God to my mom. There can be no greater honor.

Day after day I wondered how I could bring our beloved mother home. Not to my home but to her home. This was where she wanted to be. She had lived there for about fifty years. Her flowers and plants where outside and needed her attention. The breakfast table was empty and lonely without a warm body sitting at it, with a cup of coffee rattling on the top. The television in the bedroom was silent. Normally, Catherine would cozy up in bed and watch the evening news. The front porch would be inviting her to come and sit down. She could watch the neighbors come and go or the kids run up and down the street playing and hollering. The neighbors would perhaps stop at the fence or come up to the house to see how she was doing. That house would be therapy for her. She never wanted to leave there, and if she was going to die soon, she would want it to be there.

I made calls, drove places, did what I could possibly do to see if I could get her home at least one more time. Nothing worked. On top of that, I was advised that by moving her it may be too much for her body to take the transporting. It could actually kill her. Then there was the question of care. We couldn't afford twenty-four-hour care. There wasn't enough money to pay someone out of our personal resources. Every door was closed. It was very disheartening. I had heard stories of people bringing their love ones home to die, and I couldn't pull it off. I needed to be thankful for the care she was getting at the nursing home. A kind nurse, like Ruth, who took her vitals or crushed up her medicine so she could swallow it. The attendants who bathed her or wiped her when she made a bowel movement. I needed to be grateful for therapists who were trying to teach her how to swallow. Those who had to try and help her regain muscle strength. All I could do was continue getting up in the morning and make the trek to take her the oatmeal, coffee, and KFC mashed potatoes. Then come back in the afternoon or evening for some scripture reading and perhaps a stroll outside. My sister Carolyn would visit and take her clean clothes and make provisions for her hair to be done. I am sure she would say some things to make her laugh. It was also very encouraging for me when others came by to see her. They would come, talk to her, try to feed her, and pray for her.

As the days went on, there would be a couple of signs that things were getting better. When there were positive signs, I would leave after visiting, real excited. Maybe her countenance would be bright, or she ate a little more. Perhaps the nurse would say something encouraging about her progress. I would call Carolyn or Pam from the cell phone as I was walking back to the car. I would be bubbling over with excitement. The other side is that there were times that the overwhelming evidence was that she was getting worse. It got to the point where I would hate to hear the cell phone ring, believing it would only be the dreaded call: "Mister Audrick, I am sorry. She is gone."

Chapter 27
MOM, DO YOU LOVE JESUS?

O ur mother's ordeal forced me to face some serious questions: What do I really believe? What happens at death? What happens beyond death? How does one prepare for death? Catherine Anderson was heading toward the end of her life. It was becoming clearer that no matter how much I, Carolyn, or Pam prayed, or asked others to pray, our mother's life was nearing the end. My hope that my mother was going to live to see her one hundredth birthday was probably not going to be realized. She would come a few years short. It was going to be ninety-six years old rather than one hundred when my mom would stand before God. If your loved one appears to be at the end of their life, don't stop praying, hoping, and even believing for the turnaround, no matter how dire the situation appears. I am sure there are many, many testimonies from people who have seen miraculous recoveries from people at death's door.

In 1979, while in my last year of college, God intervened in my life and through another individual I was introduced to the Gospel of Jesus Christ. This gospel teaches that all men are separated from God by sin, and because of sin we are not only separated from God but can't live on in his presence after death because of sin. God, in his love for us, sent his only Son, the Lord Jesus Christ, to pay man's sin debt so we can be reconciled to him and live beyond the grave in a blessed eternal state. This certainty of victory beyond the grave is guaranteed because Jesus not only died but rose again from the grave on the third day. The Gospel teaches us very emphatically that there is only one way to gain eternal life, and that is through the Lord Jesus Christ. One must repent of sin and receive freely this precious gift of eternal life. One Sunday afternoon in 1979, I did that. From that time on—now some forty-one years later—I have believed that to be true. Yes, doubts have tried to creep in, but God will not let me forsake that blessed gospel of hope. For the past forty-one years, I have tried to share this gospel with various people as opportunity presented itself, and, of course, that includes my dear mother. If I truly believe this wonderful gospel message, it would not demonstrate much love for my mother if I didn't tell her. How could I be concerned about everyone else and ignore the very person who birthed me into this world?

I spoke earlier of my mother's spiritual journey as I understood it. It involved an early baptism, which she wanted of her own free will, and a desire to sing in the choir. None of these things make a person a Christian or guarantee eternal life. We are not saved by works of our own. Salvation is a free gift that must be received freely. But my mom might have been saved, and these desires came as a result of her salvation. Perhaps more likely these things indicated some spiritual hunger inside her. That hunger could only be satisfied upon truly experiencing forgiveness of sins and receiving God's pardon. Whatever the case, my mom shied away from discussing spiritual things, so I never really knew if she had experienced true forgiveness of sins. In her later years, she started to just show little signs that God, by his grace, was working in her life. Perhaps all the reading of scriptures and the conversations and being in the presence of God's people was starting to soften her heart. Every person, no matter how morally good they are, has to have their heart softened by God. Sometimes, when I think back over my mother's spiritual life, I wonder if her spiritual walk or life was not hindered by bitterness due to some bad life experiences. As the days went on, life expectancy was really in question.

God was being merciful. I am sure that each day of life was a miracle in and of itself. So as the days went on it became a matter of urgency that Catherine Anderson was prepared to die. The only way to be prepared to die is to know that Jesus Christ is our savior. No one should ever die without settling that question. The Bible is crystal clear. In John, chapter 14 verse 6 (NKJV), we read, "Jesus said to him, 'I am the way, the truth; and the life. No one comes to the Father except through Me.'" No water baptism. No amount of singing in the choir. No amount of works can be sufficient to grant a person eternal life. It is only by receiving the free gift of salvation purchased by the spilled blood of the Lord Jesus Christ. Unless Jesus Christ is our savior, we will be kept outside of heaven's gates for all eternity. So it became paramount to me to know where Catherine Anderson stood. Hopefully, I have made it clear on previous pages that the stroke had taken away my mother's ability to talk, swallow, or move her right side. It was hoped that as time went on she would slowly regain some of these functions. It was not to be. She never regained the use of her right side, talk or swallow. One thing I am very grateful for is that she could understand and react to instructions or commands. On a couple of occasions, I asked her to take her hand and rub my head. She would lift her left hand with amazing agility and rub my head. I don't remember my mother ever rubbing my head, but here I am, sixty-five years later, and she is tenderly rubbing my head. I would then ask her to rub my face, and again with amazing agility she would lift her left hand against my face and rub it tenderly. I wasn't asking my mom to rub my head or face to see if she could. I wanted my mom's tender affection as she lay dying on that bed. She wasn't a hugger or one to walk up to her children and plant a kiss on them. It just wasn't in her makeup, and probably not mine, although I always made sure that on certain occasions I would plant a gentle kiss on her cheek or forehead. I am pretty certain I both cried and smiled as I felt the tender rub of her hand over my head and face. Touches are very powerful words. They last only a few seconds, but they speak volumes. Although she couldn't say it, perhaps as death closed in, she wanted me to know "I love you." I am grateful for those times when we feel or sense an inward impulse to carry out a moral act. Perhaps there is a sense of urgency to it. It could be the prompting of God or some inward conscious impulse moving us forward. Whichever it is, I sensed a desire to have a spiritual conversation with Catherine Anderson. The conversation was strictly to determine if she was prepared to enter eternal life. The conversation we had on that day was only two questions and two answers. I said this to her: "Mom, do you love Jesus? If you do, blink your eyes."

She blinked.

Next question: "Mom, is Jesus your savior? If the answer is yes, squeeze my hand."

Without any hesitation, she squeezed my hand.

Some people might say the questions were not strong enough or definitive enough. Some might even say blinking or squeezing my hand were not strong answers. I would disagree with both conclusions. Those questions and answers were probing my mom's heart. God interprets what is going on in the heart—what is the true desire of the individual. It's not how correctly a question is phrased or answered. The questions centered on Jesus and him being her savior. Mom's heart had to have been broken for her to blink and squeeze my hands as her only way of communicating. She could have been bitter and refused to humble herself to acknowledge her need of a savior. In over sixty years of life, I had never heard my mom acknowledge verbally her need of a savior, but now in her silence she screamed for Jesus. Our mother did in that moment what we all must do before we die, and that is acknowledge our need for a savior, and Jesus is that savior. That my mother did. I am glad God reads blinks and hand squeezes.

Chapter 28
THE CALL

We live in the wonderful age of huge technological advances that make it nearly impossible not to be able to instantly communicate with anybody at any time in any part of the world. In the days before cell phones, social media, and personal computers, the best we could do was call from a landline or write a letter or send a telegram. Getting a message to someone was the hope that they would be near a phone or that the mail would be swiftly delivered. Boy, have we come a long way! Today we can often be in contact with anybody twenty- four hours a day within a matter of seconds. Even if someone is not technologically savvy—I fall into that camp— and they own a cell phone, they can be reached at any time of the day pretty much no matter where they are. I don't have much interest in cell phones or personal computers. I would have been okay with the continued use of landlines and writing letters. I am not a person whose life would be miserable without internet access. Having said all that, I am very grateful to have had a cell phone in my possession, since it was very important that someone be able to get in contact with me or my sister about my mom's heath, especially since it had started to deteriorate.

Of course, that cell phone allowed me to be able to check on our mother at any time, no matter where I was. I could also fill my sisters in on any information at any time. Sometimes when I would make a call to check up on her the news was not always encouraging. The attending nurse would sometimes say things like, "She isn't eating," or "She was tired." Day by day she was getting weaker, with maybe a momentary spurt of improvement here or there, but overall, she was going down.

One of the things I was doing at the time of my mom's illness was finding a quiet place near a lake or river or some outdoors place where I could sit in my car surrounded by God's beauty and read my Bible and pray. As a side note here, one of the best things one can do consistently is take some time each week, find a quiet place at a park or somewhere else, and go and absorb the quiet. I would suggest reading the Bible and talking to God in addition to absorbing the quiet. For those who don't believe in God, just meditate and sit still. Maybe in the silence God will speak. Everybody needs to come away from the noise of society, even if only for a small amount of time. On this particular day, I was at a very quiet spot in Northern Virginia. I was at a place called Turkey Run. It was a very quiet spot some fifty feet above the Potomac River. Silence filled the air. Tall, beautiful trees stood among the tranquility. Only the sound of a bird or ground animal broke the silence. There may have been the occasional car or hiker that moved across the quietness. It was perfect to open my Bible, to pray, and to cry out to God as I sat in my car. I had not been there long before the phone rang. I am sure when I heard the phone ring and saw it was from the nursing home that my heart went to a thousand beats per minute. It was

Ruth the nurse. She informed me in a soft, somewhat somber voice that Mom was getting weak. I knew it was serious and that I should get there as fast as I could. I interpreted Ruth's message to mean our mother was slipping away—that she was at death's door. I began racing down the highway, trying to call my sister at the same time. If my memory serves me correctly, it was at this time when I got there that my mom was laboring in breathing. She would take a breath, and then there would seem to be a pause before the next breath would come. At the time her right leg was kicking in and out in a slow rhythmic motion. It was very obvious death was imminent. It is surreal to witness someone dying. It was around afternoon, maybe a little earlier, when both my sister and I arrived. Not every detail of that day is fresh in my mind, but some are. My older sister Carolyn pulled up some appropriate songs on her cell phone and put them up to her mother's ear. I also remember she sang to Mom. I kidded her about not knowing she could sing so well. I am pretty sure we called my sister Pam and allowed her to tell her mother how much she loved her. Pam, her husband, her two kids, and her two grandkids had just been there a few days ago after driving about sixteen hours from Missouri. At that time, we thought Mom was at death's door and that they needed to come right away. Well, God, in his sovereignty did not allow her to die at that time. There is no doubt in my mind that Pam drove all the way back to Missouri with a very heavy heart, feeling very strongly that her mother would not be alive for long.

As our mother laid there, taking very laborious and shallow breaths, my heart was breaking. The tears would flow on and off. The words "I love you" came often. I told her that shortly she would be in heaven and that heaven was a beautiful place. I do not think I began to make a habit of saying "I love you" to my mother until later in life. I love my mother very much, but we just didn't make a habit of saying those words often. I will always believe we loved each other, but the words were very scarce. To say the words "I love you" takes practice. I wish I could have said a thousand times: "Mama, I love you."

As time went on that day, one of mom's neighbors came in. Her name was Mrs. Moore. She had befriended my mom over the years. I believe the attraction that drew them was they both had an interest in flowers and the beautification of their yards. Mrs. Moore was a kind Christian woman, and I was glad she took an interest in my mom. Catherine Anderson had very few friends over her lifetime. She found it difficult to make friends or keep them. She kept to herself, so friends came at a premium. On this day, Mrs. Moore entered the room, unbeknownst to me, as I was bent over my dying mother. She sat down beside me, grabbed my hand, and began to pray and beseech God to not let my mom die. The tears were freely falling from both our eyes as she prayed, and I agreed with her words. As I look back on that day, I wonder if we should have kept our emotions a little more in check, as I am not sure what Mom was taking in. If she was clearly hearing us, we may have been frightening her, but who knows. Sometimes our emotions are just spontaneous. They come on us without any warning. We have no time to process.

As the day went on, God was gracious. There was not a lot of people coming and going. There were no crowds around the bedside to say goodbye, just a few: my sister and I, Mrs. More, and a couple of pastor friends. The pastors came in at different times. They sat and talked awhile with me. They sang and prayed and then left. Right around five o'clock in the evening, I was getting tired, and I thought my mother was going to be alive the next day, so I decided to leave and go home. No one said different to me. Nobody tried to talk me out of it, so I left. I really don't know why I left. Maybe I thought God was going to heal my mother, or maybe I didn't understand the seriousness of her labored breathing. Perhaps I felt she would be alive in the morning. I should have set aside my tiredness and just held my mom's hand, even if for only a couple of more hours. To this day I regret not staying and being a comfort to her in the last hours of life. Obviously I don't know what the experience of dying feels like but I can imagine that it is a comfort to have people near you and consoling you as life on this earth comes to an end.

After leaving the nursing home around five pm, I had a long rush-hour drive home. I was all alone in the car with my thoughts and a crowded highway around me. Finally reaching home, talking to my lovely wife, eating dinner; sitting up for a short time, I was off to bed. While I don't remember the exact time, I don't believe I was in the bed for more than an hour when around 10pm the cell phone rang. I jumped up, saw the number, and identified the caller. It was the nursing home with the call I didn't want to hear: "I am sorry Mr. Audrick, but she is gone."

As if I didn't know what that meant, I think I remember replying, "Do you mean she is dead?"

"Yes," she replied.

I dressed and my wife and I made the long, silent drive in the dark back to the nursing home to see my deceased mother. I can't remember what the drive was like. I am pretty sure there were moments of silence, consoling words from my wife, and periods of sobs. I don't believe there was any hysteria or out-of-control sobbing. God gave me stability and a sense of peace. God will always give the grace to handle these moments of crisis.

When we arrived at the nursing home, it was quiet. There was the lady at the front desk, but there appeared to be a peacefulness to the place. There were no employees scurrying around, just quiet. We walked to the elevator and pushed for floor number two. Once off the elevator, there was what seemed like a very long walk down to my mother's room even though it was only a few doors. At one point I could see my sister Carolyn and her daughter Erika standing out in the hall. Apparently, they had already been in. Once at the door, we exchanged some words, and Frances and I went in. I sat down beside her bed in the quiet of the night and rubbed her head, kissed her, and wept. After a few moments, I got up walked out of the room. I walked down the hall to weep alone. A nurse came up to meet me who was my mother's attending nurse that night. As if to shake me out of the pity she told me in so many words to stop the crying—my mother was in heaven.

While I would never try to stop somebody from expressing a genuine emotion at the death of a loved one, we do need to be reminded that anybody who has received Jesus Christ as their savior is in heaven at the moment of their passing. That is what we, the ones left behind, need to be reminded of. "To be absent from the body is to be present with the Lord" (2 Corinthians 5:6). At the moment Catherine Anderson closed her eyes in death, she was with the Lord. Hallelujah!

Chapter 29
THE FUNERAL

T his would be the first time I was actually involved in the planning of a funeral. I would work in a joint effort with my sister Carolyn to plan out what we had hoped would be a wonderful funeral for our dear mother. This would be the one last act of kindness we could show her, even though she was not here to acknowledge it. I found out very quickly that we had to be able to grieve and yet be composed enough to handle the business side of burying a loved one. Right away I came to understand funerals were a business. The people are sympathetic to the loss, but we wouldn't get pass first base unless we had dollars. From my personal experience, there was no such thing as a payment plan. No promise to pay in the future would be acceptable. No sob story would work. Before one shovel of dirt is removed from the ground, it has to be paid in full or at least guaranteed through an insurance policy. Of course, for a lot of funeral businesses, the simple goal is to make the sale and the more expensive the better. Funeral people probably work on commission, or at least part commission and their income had a lot to do with the amount of deals they closed so I am sure there was pressure to make the sell. Mom had very little insurance, and we were very fortunate that my sister Carolyn and her husband were able to get the money together. We all wanted Catherine Anderson to have a beautiful funeral. She deserved it.

To be honest, I do not remember the sequence of events. I just know we had to find a cemetery, order a plaque, find a church, get bulletins made, assemble pictures for the bulletin, order a casket, and on and on. I do remember that with each one of these events there was a certain amount of sadness. I am sure there were times that right in the middle of discussing something with a salesperson I would begin to cry. I am all for preplanning everything out down to the repast. Have the gravesite paid for, the casket paid for, write up the obituary,; pick out the pictures; name the songs; and assign people to sing. When someone dies, the only thing the person left to bury them should have to do is call friends and loved ones. There should also be easy access to the people who need to be called. It is emotionally draining if those charged with planning the funeral have to scramble to get everything done. It can be quite taxing when the person doing the planning has to deal with his or her emotions along with the stress of planning.

I wanted everybody to know about my mother's passing and the funeral arrangements. I passed out leaflets in the neighborhood where my mother resided for at least fifty years. I went around to churches where I knew pastors and other ministers. I put up notices in the nursing home from where she departed this life. I called family members. I wanted my mom's funeral to be well attended. Our mother didn't have many friends-as I have said several times already and for whatever reason she didn't endear herself to many. Sometimes there is a lack of endearment for any of us because people form wrong judgments without really knowing us.

Catherine Anderson was my mom, and whatever had to be done so she would have a wonderful funeral I wanted to do it. Of course, the deceased is not in the body nor aware of who is attending. It could be one or one thousand, and they wouldn't know, but I still wanted our mother's funeral to be special.

People were very kind to me and my family during the planning. Many acts of kindness. My wife and I were without a church home as we had left our previous church and were in the process of looking for another. My mother did not have a church and had not been a member of one that I am aware of for all my life. Not having a church home, I went back to my old church, and they gladly let us use the church. They also provided the choir and the repast food—no charge. They showed real Christian love. My good friend from Pennsylvania drove the three hours to play the saxophone. Three pastor friends and an elder conducted the funeral. One of the unique acts of kindness was performed by some of the younger people from the neighborhood. One of the young people, with whom my mother had a running feud, consented to be one of the pallbearers. That was a really touching act for me. Here was this young man who my mother sparred with for more than a year, and now he would be one of the ones to carry her to her final resting place. It was a very touching statement. It said to me that this person respected and cared for Ms. Anderson, even though the way they battled, one would have thought they detested each other. Then a couple of other neighbors volunteered to help in some way. Mom was the neighborhood watchman. If kids were acting out of line, she made it known their behavior was unacceptable. Suspicious activity in the neighborhood? She was on top of it. She was fearless. So, although she was despised by some who wanted her quiet, she would now be the recipient of kindness from some of those same people. A few other people volunteered to say a kind word for my mother. One of the people who spoke was a manager at a food co-op. Over the last ten years or so of my mother's life, she was really into eating right and taking her supplements. She frequented this particular store once a month and had been made to feel really welcomed. The week my mother died, I went up to that store and cried like a baby when I told the manager. I asked if they would send someone to say a word for my mother, and they did. Three people actually came and also brought flowers. People sent cards and gave money. Overall, there was a genuine spirit of kindness.

After a couple of weeks of planning and making arrangements and being emotionally spent, the day of the funeral finally came. My siblings and their families, along with my wife and I, planned to meet at my mom's house. How surreal it was to be standing in the house that had been filled with Catherine Anderson's footsteps. We waited patiently for the family car. There wasn't much sitting down. I am sure there was walking back and forth between the kitchen, dining room, and living room. As we walked, our thoughts wondered into the past sounds and scenes of this house. As we waited, there was small talk mixed with laughter and tears. The laughter only masked the brokenness of our hearts. Time seemed to drag on for what appeared to be hours as we waited for this shiny blue car to usher us to the church. I guess the day I never dreamed of happening was going to be happening in a very short amount of time. It was always somebody else's mother who was being buried. My mother was going to live to be a hundred. Reality had set in. What had happened to others was now happening to me and my siblings. It was all so surreal, sitting there in that small living room, sometimes laughing, sometimes crying as we waited for the family car. I remember the streets were quiet on that early morning around nine o'clock. I feel pretty confident in saying that there were people peeping out their windows, waiting to see the family emerge and slide into that limousine off to bury Ms. Catherine Anderson, the resident who had lived at 4207 H Street for about fifty years. No longer would they see that small-framed woman stand on the porch with a cup of coffee in her hands, peering up and down the street. No longer would they see Catherine Anderson out in her front yard, puttering around with her flowers or watering her grass. She was gone. The house was empty, and only silence would reside there until new tenants arrived.

Right on time, this beautiful blue limo pulled up. The driver, very pleasant, got out and helped us in. My wife and I and my two sisters and their husbands rode in the limo. The others took their personal cars. The car drove off slowly down H Street, took the first left, and began to leave the neighborhood. The tears rolled down. As we drove on, I surveyed other cars and the surroundings, with my thoughts definitely on my precious mom. I have lived in Washington, DC, and its surrounding areas for about sixty-five years at the time of this writing, but everything seemed like a fog to me. Our location didn't make much sense to me as we drove slowly along. I just peered aimlessly out the window of the limo and only noticed streets that appeared to be empty. It seemed that silence was the only noise I heard. What should have been a normal twenty-minute drive seemed to take longer. I am sure it was because the driver drove a little slower out of respect to the family.

Finally, we pulled up to the church, a little old gray stone building. It was a bit run down. There were stairs to climb to get into the sanctuary—no elevator. There was a sharp bend in the steps, so the casket needed to be carried up through the back of the church, where it was a straight shot. This was the church where my wife and I had been members for fifteen years. I was an associate minister there for those fifteen years. After having left, we had not been back for a church service but were now coming back to bury my mother. The people of this church, as I previously mentioned, were very gracious to me. The church was opened, and everything was in place to give our mom a dignified service. The viewing would be from ten to eleven, and the service itself would be from eleven to noon.

Exiting the car, we walked a few feet to the door and climbed the stairs of the old church to enter the unassuming sanctuary, where my beloved mother laid silently in the casket. As I remember, there were no people there at this early moment other than my immediate family, maybe a couple of ushers, and the pallbearers. I went up to the casket to view my mom and right away I was struck by how beautiful and peaceful she looked. Of course, I was well aware that the face I had looked at for over sixty years was unaware that I was there. She could not respond to my tears. She wouldn't react to the kiss I planted on her forehead or the gentle rub of my hand against hers. No, her frail, sickened body laid helplessly in that beautiful casket while the real Catherine Anderson had taken flight and went home to be with her Lord and Savior.

As time went on, the church became alive as people came in to say goodbye and to show respect to our beloved mother and family. As more and more people came in, my heart was made glad. There were people I knew and people I didn't know. There were people I knew but didn't expect to see at the service. There were neighbors and friends of my two sisters. There were other family members. There were clergy and deacons. All told, approximately seventy- five people were in attendance. To me, it seemed like a thousand. Perhaps we wondered who would come outside of the immediate family, but God was gracious. As a matter of fact, I might have only had seventy-five programs printed, and they were gone, and we might have needed more, so maybe we were approaching the one-hundred mark.

Eleven o'clock came, and if I remember correctly, the ministers entered the pulpit, and the first order of business was to allow the family one last look at the beloved deceased. We gathered at the open casket for one final gaze into our mother's face. This would be the last time we would gather around her. Once that casket was closed, we would only have memories. The service began, and it proceeded much the same as any other funeral. Just a couple of things to point out: The saxophonist played "Swing Low, Sweet Chariot" and "Amazing Grace." Two ministers read an Old and a New Testament reading. My mom's favorite scripture, Psalm 91, was read and then a portion of 1 Corinthians 15—concerning the promise of the bodily resurrection—was read. The pastor delivered a wonderful message that was salvation based. The choir sang a couple of songs. A few people spoke some beautiful words about my mom, and before we knew it was time to move on to the actual interment.

Who enjoys a long ride in a limousine to a cemetery to bury a loved one? I don't know of anyone. There we were, taking that slow ride from Washington, DC, to Suitland, Maryland, for the purpose of laying to rest our dearly beloved Catherine Anderson. I imagine it was about a thirty-minute ride to the cemetery. All along our thoughts were in wonder mode. We were looking at all the people and cars. Those who we passed along the way were oblivious to the sadness we were experiencing. They were probably paying no attention, with the exception of those who were being held up because our funeral procession was passing through their intersection.

Finally, we made the slow turn into the cemetery. A car was waiting to lead us to the plot where Mama would be buried. Within a few minutes, we were there, the last leg of the journey. God had blessed my mom with a wonderful spot. It was only about ten feet off the road, under a wonderful shade tree. Whenever we go to visit her grave, it is less than a fifteen-second walk to her grave, and no matter how hot it is we have some protection from the sun. We don't often think about or appreciate these little gifts from God, but we should. At the end of each day, if we would just look back, we would see little blessings sprinkled along the way, like rose petals scattered along the ground.

The graveside service was not very long. There was a reading of a small part of 1 Corinthians 15. There were some words spoken by the pastor and a committal of the body to the earth. After the committal of the body back to the ground, there were well-wishes and hugs. People engaged in talk and some laughter. I remember standing over the casket, along with other members of the family and my memories. There were the soft sobs from my nephew and some precious remarks by my niece and some reflection by myself and others. Soon it was time to leave the body of Catherine Anderson and carry with us only our precious memories. Within a short time, we were back at the church to enjoy a nice repast prepared by the people of this church. After a short repast, it was time to leave—time to go home to be alone with our thoughts. Time to begin a life that would never again involve a conversation with our very precious mother, Catherine Anderson. There would be no phone call the next day asking, "What are you doing?" No voice asking, "What did Frances fix for dinner?" There would be no need for me to stop over to see how she was doing. The reality was that it was time to move forward with a life that would not include Ms. Catherine Anderson.

Chapter 30
MOVING FORWARD

eath, for all of us, is a separation. It is a breaking of a bond. For some, it is a bond loosely held. For others, it is a bond tightly held. No matter what type of bond characterizes the relationship, it is still a separation. Every one of us one day will experience that ultimate separation. There are some separations that are temporal. They can be put back together. Two friends break up, and they separate. Perhaps at some point later in life they realize the breakup was silly, and they are rejoined as friends. A husband and wife not really understanding the covenant relationship of marriage separate and end up getting a divorce. Sometime down the road, after some very wise council, they may reconcile. On earth, death is a permanent separation. No matter how much we miss a person or long to be in their presence, it is impossible. The only thing we have are memories. We can never touch, hug, or speak to that individual again. The only thing we can do, and the most reasonable thing to do, is move on. Please do not think when I say move on that I am saying, "Pull yourself together! Shape up! Leave the past! Forget the past." No, to move on involves different things for different people, but generally it should mean to continue your life's journey. Some people refuse to move on because they feel as though when the life of their beloved stops their' also stops. We need to understand that one of the most significant ways we honor our deceased is to move on. They would want us to fulfill our purpose and calling in this life, especially if they were an integral part of that purpose and calling . There are, I am sure, many people who in the face of imminent death encouraged those who would be left behind to move forward with their goals, dreams, and life in general. How many stories have we heard of a husband or wife on their deathbed encouraging their spouses to remarry. Those departing this life would not want our lives to be miserable and unfulfilling just because they couldn't be a part of it. Catherine Anderson I believe was no different-she would want her children and grandchildren to move forward. She would want us to live out our days by being productive. She would want us to pursue a life that was better than hers. In general she would want us to achieve everything that God would allow.

While I can't provide a day-by-day accounting of my life after my mother's funeral, I can provide some broad chunks. While I loved my mother dearly and miss her sorely, even as I write this book, God protected me from a deep dark hole called depression. Some may be under the erroneous conclusion that if one is not in a state of depression, then they really didn't love the individual. All I can say is that I didn't enter the dark hole of depression, and yet I can say the tears flowed before my mother's passing. They flowed after her passing, and even now, when I talk about her to others, my eyes can well up. There were many times before her passing that I would get in my car and go off to a quiet place and talk to God about healing her. There were many times after her passing when I would get in my car and go to a place of solace, where I could talk to God about my mom. The conversations I had with God about her are private, but I am sure I have asked God on more than one occasion to tell her that I love her.

One of the other emotional events occurring after my mother's passing was the selling of the house and getting rid of everything in it.. The easiest thing to have done would have been to call a professional service to come and clean out the house, trashing everything in it. I did not want that to happen. Whatever was in that house, no matter how old and dusty, it represented either what my mom worked hard to obtain, or someone had given it to her. To me, I wanted to either sell it or give it away. If it was sold, the money could be used to pay off a bill of hers or perhaps split it among the grandkids. If it was given away, then somewhere, in some part of the Maryland, DC, Virginia area, someone would be benefitting from her possessions. She could still be a blessing, even in death. One of the real special giveaways was when I took some of my mom's clothes to an organization that gave away professional-looking clothes to needy women who had nothing to wear on job interviews. I walked into the establishment with the offer of some of my mom's really nice clothing. After looking over the generous offering, I was told that some of the things they couldn't take because there was a certain style that was needed. For some reason, I had brought along a pullover shirt with a picture of President Obama on it. Our mother used to wear that shirt quite a bit. She was quite proud of the first African American president. There was a lady working at this establishment who I believed to be the supervisor. She was white and had an eighth-grade daughter who was really fond of President Obama. After a conversation and some tears, I convinced her to take the shirt and give it to her daughter. She consented with some reservation, as she didn't want to take away something that was obviously very meaningful to my mother. She indicated she would put it aside and give it to her daughter as a present on an upcoming birthday. I made only one request: that she send me a picture of her daughter wearing it. That she did. That was one of the special moments I had as we sold or gave away everything in Mom's house. Nothing was to go in the trash. Somebody somewhere could use the things at 4207 H Street.

The day finally came when the house was emptied, cleaned, and sold. That single-family brick home that became our prized possession, the house we were associated with for fifty years, the house our mother labored so hard to purchase, was gone. The only thing that will be in that house forever are the memories. It was a moment of detachment. I could drive by that house, but I would never see my mom standing on the porch and talking to a neighbor or just looking over the neighborhood. I could drive by that house but never stop and walk up to the front door, open it with a key, and enter. My detachment from the house has not been without its temptations. There have been a few times when I have yielded to the desire to go over and look at the house. I have driven over to see what changes the new owner has made. One time I drove to the back of the house, which can be accessed by an alley. I noticed he had taken down the fence and put an area for a barbeque grill. The flowers in the front yard were still there. A new brick wall replaced the tattered front fence. I took a momentary gaze at the new front windows that my mom had paid for. Boy, there are stories behind how our mother had to dig deep to pay for those,- in my mind,- very expensive windows, along with a very expensive new front storm door. From what I understand, the owner did some interior renovations that changed some of the house's original character. Every time I drive by the old house, I slow down to take a quick look. I try not to stop and stare. Too many emotions are stored up at the house I had known for almost fifty years.

One day I would like to buy back that house at 4207 H Street. We had to sell the house to reimburse Carolyn and her husband (which was the only right thing to do), who had surrendered thousands of dollars of their financial resources to pay for the funeral. That really is not what she wanted, but none of us had the money to pay for her funeral, so the house was sold. I have asked God about allowing me the opportunity to buy the house back. I feel it should be left in the family, and maybe one day after we are gone from this earth, the generations that follow can use it or sell it if they choose. Of course, at our age, this dream of mine would have to be an act of God. We are in no position, naturally speaking, to purchase that house, but God is able.

From the time I was about twenty-five years old up until my mom's passing, I had always tried to do things with her—take her places, mostly within the DC metropolitan area, or on short two- or three-hour trips. We would also go out to dinner or breakfast, go on picnics, or go sightseeing. At other times, there would be things of a more spiritual nature. I always, though not perfectly, tried to involve her in activities that got her out of the house and into other parts of the world. There were many other places I wanted to take her—many other things I wanted to do with her. I find myself often remarking to my wonderful wife, Frances, about places and things I wish Mama got to see. We may be driving past a restaurant, and I will say, "I was going to take my mother there." In the back of my mind, there still seems to be soom unfinished business. Maybe it is here I can offer a piece of sound advice: we should do as much as possible with our loved ones before they are gone. Don't keep putting things off. Death has a way of catching us off guard. Don't store up dreams and wishes to rust. Once our loved ones are gone, dreams and wishes are just that—dreams and wishes.

Part of moving forward for me is taking time on all those special days, like Mother's Day, Christmas, and birthdays, to visit her grave and try to adorn it with special flowers. I generally pay attention to the graves of others as I drive up on the grounds and notice how they are decorated. Not everybody visits their beloveds' graves. The indication of that is that there are no flowers, and the grave looks very untidy. Some people, for whatever reason, just don't bother to visit. I don't want to assume that if a person doesn't visit someone's grave on various occasions that they somehow don't love them. On the other hand, I normally read into all the beautiful flowers and balloons on the graves as an indication that the person in the grave is greatly missed and loved. I don't know how long I will be doing it, but it has been three years since my mother's passing, and maybe only once or twice have I missed taking flowers to her grave on those special occasions. I don't say this as some sort of self-righteous act or to pat myself on the back, but something inside me feels like this is a way to honor her. I want the grass on her grave to be well kept and flowers to decorate it. I want people to know that Catherine Anderson was a special mom. I don't want her grave to be dark and barren, as if no one cared. Not only do I consider it a blessing to be able to take flowers to the grave, but I try to spend a little time there in reflection and prayer and perhaps read some scripture. One thing I don't do is try to talk to her. No one is in the grave. The body that housed the person is there, but the actual person has departed. On June 9, 2017, my mom departed her body and went home to be with her Lord. The physical body is in the grave rotting, but because we are physical beings we associate with the physical world. I understand that I will never see her again as she looked on earth, but one day she will be resurrected from the grave with a brand-new imperishable body that will be nothing like the human body that was decayed and broken down. In 1 Corinthians, chapter 15 verse 51–54 (NKJV), we read, "Behold I tell you a mystery: We shall not all sleep, but we shall all be changed—in a moment, in the twinkling of an eye, at the last trumpet. For the trumpet will sound, and the dead will be raised incorruptible, and we shall be changed. For this corruptible must put on incorruption, and this mortal must put on immortality. So, when this corruptible has put on immortality then shall be brought to pass the saying that is written: 'Death has been swallowed up in victory.'"

I don't really know how things work in heaven. I know it is a place beyond any beauty we can imagine. I know it is an actual physical place, where the people of God will experience true, eternal prosperity. I know God is there. It is a place of indescribable worship. It is a place of innumerable people of every race and ethnicity, but heaven is so much more than that. There is so much that we can't understand about heaven and the new earth that God will prepare for us. People often ask, "Will we know each other?" While I am not qualified to answer that question, I do know our relationships will not be the same. For example, there will be no marriage in heaven, so husbands will not be scouring heaven for their lovely wives so they can carry on the idyllic and blissful marriage they had on earth. While I don't know all the things that will take place in heaven, I hope I can meet my mother again, throw my arms around her, and say, "Thank you, Mom. I love you so very much."

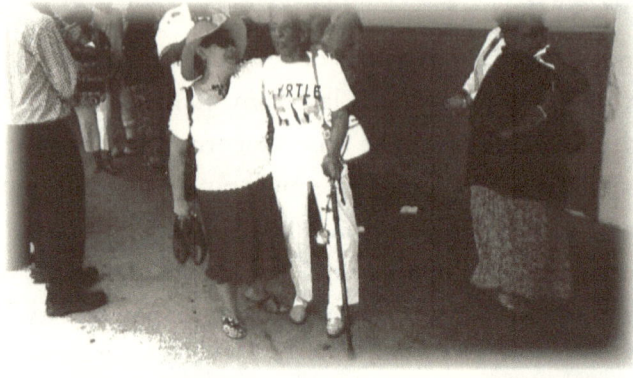

As I noted in various places throughout the book, our mother didn't have many friends. One here and one there. Not only that, but the friendships also never seemed to last. So, for sure there were long periods of loneliness and isolation. Approximately two years before my mother died, we went on a luncheon cruise that lasted about two hours. Upon getting off the boat God seemed to drop a friend down from heaven. Within a few minutes of talking and laughing, my mom and her new found friend walk off into the sunset arms around each other. I have many pictures of my mom but the one above may be my favorite. Thank you, God, for my mom's new found friend."

EPILOGUE

They May Never Know You

Catherine Anderson, the world may never know you.

They may never know about your body, weakened by years of hard work.

They may never know about the endless love you had for your family.

They may never know about your determined spirit, fighting to give us a chance in life.

No, you were not a famous actress. No, you were not a famous doctor. No, you were not a famous politician. No, you were not rich and famous.

No, you are not mentioned in any history book.

They may never know you.

They may never know about all the sleepless nights, wondering about your children.

They may never know how endless hours of worry contributed to the wrinkles

They may never know of the long bus rides to clean the homes of others.

They may never know how you denied yourself even the smallest desires of your heart.

They may never hear your prayers asking God to bless us.

They may never know how you were sometimes misunderstood, but persevered.

They may never know how you were sometimes misunderstood, but still cared.

They may never know how you were sometimes misunderstood, but still loved.

They may never know how you were sometimes misunderstood, but still selfless.

"No, I am not perfect," you would say. "No, my life was not easy," you would say.

"No, I'm not going to ever give up, no matter the circumstances," you would say.

They may never know your occasional belly laughs, which allowed you a respite.

They may never know your courage as you stood between harm and your children.

They may never know your courage as you withstood those who sought evil.

They may never know of the sage advice you gave to your kids.

They may never know of the ninety-six years of longevity that God gave you on this earth.

They may never know of the massive stroke in year ninety-six.

They may never know that the stroke would never allow you to talk with your kids again.

They may never know your silent thoughts as you laid at death's door.

They may never know of your beauty as you laid silently in the coffin.

They may never know of the kind words spoken at your funeral.

They may never know of the beautiful words written on your gravestone.

They may never know you. I want them to know you.

This book will hopefully help them know Ms. Catherine Anderson.

PSALM 91 NKJV

1He who dwells in the secret place of the Most High
Shall abide under the shadow of the Almighty.

2I will say of the LORD, *"He is* my refuge and my fortress;
My God, in Him I will trust."

3Surely He shall deliver you from the snare of the fowler
And from the perilous pestilence.

4He shall cover you with His feathers,
And under His wings you shall take refuge;
His truth *shall be your* shield and buckler.

5You shall not be afraid of the terror by night,
Nor of the arrow *that* flies by day,

6*Nor* of the pestilence *that* walks in darkness,
Nor of the destruction *that* lays waste at noonday.

7A thousand may fall at your side,
And ten thousand at your right hand;
But it shall not come near you.

8Only with your eyes shall you look,
And see the reward of the wicked.

9Because you have made the LORD, *who is* my refuge,
Even the Most High, your dwelling place,

10No evil shall befall you,
Nor shall any plague come near your dwelling;

11For He shall give His angels charge over you,
To keep you in all your ways.

12In *their* hands they shall bear you up,
Lest you dash your foot against a stone.

13You shall tread upon the lion and the cobra,
The young lion and the serpent you shall trample underfoot.

14"Because he has set his love upon Me,
therefore I will deliver him;
I will set him on high, because he has known My name.

15He shall call upon Me, and I will answer him;
I *will be* with him in trouble;
I will deliver him and honor him.

16With long life I will satisfy him,
And show him My salvation."

ACKNOWLEDGMENTS

I wish to publicly thank the following people for their contributions to this book:

1. The Lord God: I am thankful for the mind and ability granted me to write this book. He said, "For without Me you can do nothing" (John 15:5 NKJV).

2. My lovely wife, Frances, who is my best friend. She never threw cold water on my enthusiasm for this book, always encouraging me to move forward and that the book will do well.

3. Ms. Tempie Beaman, who graciously agreed to read the original manuscript and offer suggestions.

4. Ms. Deborah Etheridge. My computer skills are very poor. I couldn't create files for the chapters, cut and paste things, or format the material in a proper way to submit the manuscript to the publishers. Deborah came over many times and patiently did these things on the computer for me.

5. Ms. Jania Brown: At one point my book was lost on the computer. I couldn't find it; therefore I couldn't make corrections and resubmit the manuscript for a second round of editing. I was totally frustrated. Jania came over and used her very good computer skills to locate the book and set me up so I could make necessary corrections and send the file as an email attachment.

6. Finally, a hearty thank-you to West Bow Press for their patience with me.

A NOTE FROM THE AUTHOR

I am sure many of you who read this book have special feelings about your own mothers. I would like to read a few lines of your story. Any comments about this book would be welcome too. Please feel free to send all correspondence to raudrick@verizon. net or visit www.facebook.com/reginaldaudrick.author Thank you in advance.